RUNNERS CORPORATION

SIXTH EDITION

A MERCHANDISE DISTRIBUTOR PRACTICE SET

Completed
Manually:
General Journal or Special Journals
Or
Computer:
PH General Ledger Software,
QuickBooks Pro 2008 or 2009,
Peachtree Complete Accounting 2008 or 2009

Janet Horne

Dedicated to my husband and our sons.

VP/ Publisher: Natalie E. Anderson
AVP Executive Editor: Jodi McPherson
Editorial Project Manager: Rebecca Knauer
Production Project Manager: Carol O'Rourke
Operations Specialist: Nick Sklitsis

10   9   8   7   6   5   4   3   2   1

ISBN-13: 978-0-13-606483-1
ISBN-10: 0-13-606483-3

TABLE OF CONTENTS

PREFACE

Welcome Students and Instructors!

Runners Corporation was written to provide the accounting student with an overview of how the manual concepts taught in the introductory accounting classes can be applied within a manual or computerized accounting environment. The book is written using instructions for PH General Ledger Software, Peachtree Complete Accounting 2008 or 2009, and QuickBooks Pro 2008 or 2009. This will allow the student to apply concepts learned to computerized accounting programs that are available to businesses.

The book contains information regarding using Windows but does not attempt to teach those skills in a comprehensive manner. It is presumed that the user has the basic accounting skills taught in the first accounting course. The activities will require the use of the company data files available from Prentice Hall.

Suggested Sequence

The following chart summaries the computerized accounting materials contained in the text and suggests the order in which they would best be assigned.

Assignment

1. Chapter 1 – Company History

2. Appendix A - Forms

3. Chapter 2 - General Instructions (Manual Approach)

4. Chapter 3 - Computerizing Runners Corporation using PH General Ledger Software

5. Chapter 4 - Computerizing Runners Corporation using QuickBooks Pro 2008 or 2009

6. Chapter 5 – Computerizing Runners Corporation using Peachtree Complete 2008 or 2009

7. Appendix B - Working with PH General Ledger Software, QuickBooks Pro 2008 or 2009 and Peachtree Complete 2008 or 2009

8 Appendix D - Correcting Transactions using PH General Ledger Software QuickBooks Pro 2008 or 2009 and Peachtree Complete 2008 or 2009

9. Appendix C – How to Repeat or Restart an Assignment using PH General Ledger, QuickBooks Pro 2008 or 2009 and Peachtree Complete 2008 or 2009 software

Runners Corporation

CHAPTER 1

The Company History

Runners Corporation was incorporated in the State of Washington two years ago. The corporation distributes running shoes to retailers around the United States.
Runners Corporation currently maintains a manual accounting system and uses specialized journals to record its business transactions. A general ledger is maintained, as are an accounts receivable ledger and an accounts payable ledger. Financial statements are prepared at the end of each month, and the books are closed on December 31.

This computerized practice set illustrates the general accounting principles for a corporation. The practice set will address both the manual and computerized steps to maintain the accounting system for Runners Corporation.

An Introduction to Computers

Accounting procedures are essentially the same whether they are performed manually or on a computer. The following is a list of the accounting cycle steps in a manual accounting system as compared to the steps in a computerized accounting system.

STEPS OF THE ACCOUNTING CYCLE	
Manual Accounting System	**Computerized Accounting System**
1. Business transactions occur and generate source documents.	1. Business transactions occur and generate source documents.
2. Analyze and record business transactions in a manual journal.	2. Analyze and enter business transactions in a computerized journal.
3. Post or transfer information from journal to ledger.	3. Computer automatically posts information from journal to ledger.
4. Prepare a trial balance.	4. Trial balance is prepared automatically.
5. Prepare a worksheet.	5. Enter necessary adjustments directly.
6. Prepare financial statements.	6. Financial statements are prepared automatically.
7. Journalize and post adjusting entries.	7. Completed prior to preparation of financial statements.
8. Journalize and post closing entries.	8. Closing procedures are completed automatically.
9. Prepare a post-closing trial balance.	9. Trial balance is automatically prepared as needed.

The accounting cycle comparison shows that the accountant's task of initially analyzing business transactions in terms of debits and credits (both routine business transactions and adjusting entries) is required in both manual and computerized accounting systems. However, in a computerized accounting system, the "drudge" work of posting transactions, creating and completing worksheets and financial statements, and performing the closing procedures is all handled automatically. In some computerized accounting programs, entries may also be entered on business forms and the computer will show the entry in debit/credit format when viewing the Journal.

In addition, computerized accounting systems can perform accounting procedures at greater speeds and with greater accuracy than can be achieved in a manual accounting system. It is important to recognize, however, that the computer is only a tool that can accept and process information supplied by the accountant. Each business transaction and adjusting entry must first be analyzed and recorded in a computerized journal correctly; otherwise, the financial statements generated by the computerized accounting system will contain errors and will not be useful to the business.

Before a business can begin to use a computerized accounting system, it must have the following items in place:
1. A computer system
2. Computer software
    a. Operating system software such as Windows
    b. Accounting Software such as
        1.) PH General Ledger Software
        2.) QuickBooks Pro 2008 or 2009, or
        3.) Peachtree Complete 2008 or 2009.

The Accounting Records for Runners Corporation

The business transactions completed during the first eleven months of the current year have been recorded by Runners Corporation's former bookkeeper in the general ledger. You have been hired to complete the accounting work for December 20XX and to prepare the financial statements for the year.

All beginning balances for each general ledger account, customers and vendors have been entered. The opening Trial Balance as of December 1, 20XX is displayed on the following page:

Runners Corporation
Trial Balance
December 1, 20XX

Acct. No.	Account Title	Debit	Credit
10100	Cash	$ 56,386	
10500	Marketable Securities	20,000	
11000	Accounts Receivable	47,839	
11100	Allowance for Uncollectible Accounts		$ 4,500
11500	Inventory	20,595	
11700	Prepaid Insurance	250	
11900	Office Supplies	2,000	
16000	Land	10,000	
17000	Building	150,000	
17500	Accumulated Depreciation-Building		7,500
18000	Office Equipment	42,675	
18500	Accumulated Depreciation-Office Equipment		8,535
19000	Organization Costs	5,000	
20100	Accounts Payable		56,803
20200	Income Tax Payable		
20300	Salaries Payable		
20400	Cash Dividends Payable		
20500	Interest Payable		
20600	Note Payable		
20700	Property Tax Payable		
30100	Common Stock		100,000
30200	Premium on Common Stock		
35000	Retained Earnings, January 1, 2009		68,662
36000	Donated Capital		
41000	Sales		475,445
41500	Sales Discounts	4,000	
41600	Sales Returns and Allowances	2,000	
41700	Gain on Sale of Marketable Securities		
51000	Cost of Goods Sold	206,000	
60100	Salaries Expense	133,685	
60200	Utilities Expense	3,000	
60300	Office Supplies Expense	2,000	
60400	Advertisement Expense	7,000	
60500	Depreciation Expense-Office Equipment		
60600	Depreciation Expense-Building		
60700	Insurance Expense	2,750	
60800	Uncollectible Accounts Expense	4,500	
60900	Property Tax Expense	1,665	
61000	Miscellaneous Expense	100	
61200	Interest Expense		
61300	Amortization of Organization Costs		
61400	Income Tax		
		$721,445	$721,445

The Accounts Receivable and Accounts Payable Beginning balances for December 1, 20XX appear below:

Accounts Receivable

Customer Number	Customer	Date of Invoice	Invoice Number	Amount
2050	Tog Sport Shop 2000 2nd Avenue Woodinville, WA 98072	Feb. 1	6030	$ 2,000
2052	Active Sporting Stores 65 Roosevelt Way Seattle, WA 98104	Nov. 1	6180	28,689
2055	True Sports Shop 126 12th Avenue South Seattle, WA 98107			
2056	All Sporting 200 Mercer Street Mercer Island, WA 98040	Nov. 1	6192	4,000
2057	Home Shoes Center 140 Lake Hills Bellevue, WA 98009	Nov. 1	6189	13,150
2058	String Stores 1000 1st Avenue Seattle, WA 98104			
				$47,839

Accounts Payable

Vendor Number	Vendor	Date of Invoice	PO/Invoice Number	Amount
01	Tice Manufacturing Company 200 Westlake Avenue Los Angeles, CA 90015			
02	Hay Manufacturing Company 100 Marine Park View New York, NY 10024	Nov. 17	3533	$33,000
03	Hoot Manufacturing Company 300 Sutter Street Los Angeles, CA 90015	Nov. 17	3532	$18,000
04	Say Manufacturing Company 400 Bancroft Avenue New York, NY 10024	Nov. 17	3534	$ 5,803
05	Tic Manufacturing Company 132 NE 5th Los Angeles, CA 90015			
				$56,803

To Complete the Practice Set Manually:

Review the beginning balances in the general ledger accounts, accounts receivable ledger, and accounts payable ledger. Refer to Appendix A for accounting forms to verify balances using the manual approach.

To Complete the Practice Set Using Computerized Accounting Software:

You will use one of the following software programs to complete the computerized practice set: PH General Ledger, Peachtree Complete 2008 or 2009 or QuickBooks Pro 2008 or 2009. Refer to Appendix B through D respectively to become familiar with the specific software desktop environment and installation of data files. If you are using PH General Ledger Software, go to Chapter 3 to begin entering transactions for Runners Corporation; for QuickBooks Pro 2008 or 2009 go to chapter 4; and for Peachtree Complete 2008 or 2009, go to Chapter 5. When entering data using a computer, you must use an actual year in the transaction. In the practice set the year 2009 will be used, however, use whatever year your professor requires.

Runners Corporation

CHAPTER 2

General Instructions

Runners Corporation maintains the following basic account records. All forms are found in Appendix A. Use the current year rather than 20XX when recording the transactions.

If you are instructed to enter the transactions entirely in the General Journal and post to the General Ledger accounts, you will use the following forms in Appendix A:

> General Journal (used for entering all business transactions)
> General Ledger (used for posting the business transactions)
> Accounts receivable ledger
> Accounts payable ledger
> Worksheet for the year ended December 31, 20XX
> Financial statements:
> * Income statement
> * Statement of Retained Earnings
> * Balance Sheet
> * Statement of cash flows
> Post-closing trial balance, December 31, 20XX

If you are instructed to use Special Journals for recording transactions you will use the following:

> Sales journal (sales on credit terms)
> Purchases journal (purchases made on credit terms)
> Cash receipts journal (all collections of cash)
> Cash disbursements journal (all payments of cash by check)
> General journal (all business transactions that will not be accommodated by one of the other four journals)
> General ledger (posting the business transactions)
> Accounts receivable ledger
> Accounts payable ledger
> Worksheet for the year ended December 31, 20XX
> Financial statements:
> * Income statement
> * Statement of Retained Earnings
> * Balance Sheet
> * Statement of cash flows
> Post-closing trial balance, December 31, 20XX

Narrative of December Business Transactions

Record these business transactions in the appropriate journals. Use the account titles that appear in the December 1, 20XX trial balance (page2) and the general ledger (Appendix A).

Date	Transaction
20XX Dec. 1	Received a check from Active Sporting Stores, customer number 2052, for $28,689 in full settlement of the account. (Notes: Compare Active's check with the amount in Active's subsidiary accounts receivable ledger account. If the check received pays the customer's account in full, indicate this by entering a zero in the balance column of each account. Next, enter the amount of the check in the cash receipts journal, recording a sales discount if applicable. Write the name of the customer in the Account Credited column. Since the remittance has already been posted to Active's account in the subsidiary accounts receivable ledger, place a check mark in the posting reference column of the cash receipts journal.)
Dec. 1	Borrowed $40,000 from State Bank resulting in a 10-year note payable bearing 12% interest, payable semiannually on June 1 and December 1.
Dec. 1	Issue Check # 500 to The Runners Newspaper for $200 for newspaper advertising.
Dec. 2	Sold merchandise on account to String Stores, customer number 2058. The sales invoice is number 6202 and is for $4,000, terms 1/10 n/30. Runners Corporation uses a perpetual inventory system and therefore records the cost of merchandise sold as well as the sale. Items sold: Item # 105 – 40 pairs @ 75.00 Item # 130 – 20 pairs @ 50.00 Cost of Sale: Item # 105 – 40 pairs @ 25.00 Item # 130 – 20 pairs @ 19.95 (Notes: Most of Runners Corporation's sales are on a credit basis due to the nature of the business. Record the credit sale in the sales journal. Use the sales invoice to post directly to the account of String Stores in the subsidiary accounts receivable ledger. Make a check mark in the posting reference column of the sales journal to indicate that the sales invoice has been posted to the individual account of String Stores.
Dec. 2	Purchased merchandise on account from Tice Manufacturing Company, vendor number 1. The purchase invoice is number 3356 for $8,464, terms net 30. Items purchased: Item #130—400 pairs @ 19.95 Item #120 – 22 pairs @ 22.00
Dec 3	Sold merchandise on account; invoice number 6203, to True Sports Shop, customer number 2055, for $30,000. Terms of the sale were 1/10 n/30. Items sold: Item #130 – 200 pairs @ 50.00 Item #120 – 100 pairs @ 65.00 Item #110 – 150 pairs @ 90.00 Cost of Sale: Item #130 – 200 pairs @ 19.95 Item #120 – 100 pairs @ 22.00 Item #110 – 150 pairs @ 35.00

Date	Transaction
Dec. 6	Sold merchandise to S.T. Sporting for cash, $18,500, check no. 481. Items sold: Item #105 – 100 pairs @ 75.00 Item #110 – 50 pairs @ 90.00 Item #120 – 100 pairs @65.00 Cost of Sale: Item #105 – 100 pairs @25.00 Item #110 – 50 pairs @ 35.00 Item #120 – 100 pairs @ 22.00
Dec. 8	Sold merchandise to North Shoes, located at 105 NE 8th, Bellevue, WA 98009, customer number 2062, for $2,500. The sales invoice number is 6204. Terms 1/10 n/30. Item sold: Item #130 – 50 pairs @ 50.00 Cost of Sale: Item #130 – 50 pairs @ 19.95
Dec. 8	Received a check no. 255 from All Sporting, customer number 2056, for $4,000 in payment of invoice number 6192.
Dec. 9	Received check 898 from String Stores, customer number 2058, for $3,960. The invoice number is 6202, and a sales discount of $40 was taken.
Dec. 9	Purchased merchandise from Tic Manufacturing Company, vendor number 5. The purchase invoice is number 3538 for $23,350. Terms 30 days. Items purchased: Item #105 – 400 pairs @ 25.00 Item #110 – 350 pairs @ 35.00 Item #120 – 50 pairs @ 22.00
Dec. 9	Returned $1,300 worth of merchandise to Say Manufacturing Company, vendor 4. Received a credit memorandum acknowledging a reduction in the liability account of $1,300. Item returned: Item #105 – 52 pairs @ 25.00
Dec 10	Received check 305 from True Sports Shop, customer number 2055, for $29,700 in payment of invoice number 6203, sales discount $300.
Dec. 10	Sold merchandise to Hales Sporting Goods for cash, $9,750. Items sold: Item #105—130 pairs @ 75.00 Cost of Sale: Item #105—130 pairs @ 25.00
Dec. 13	Issue Check # 501 to Hoot Manufacturing, vendor number 3, for $18,000 in payment of purchase invoice number 3532.
Dec. 14	Received $70,000 for the sale of 50,000 shares of $1 par value common stock.
Dec. 15	Received check 678 from North Shoes, customer number 2062, for $2,475, invoice number 6204. A sales discount of $25 was taken by North Shoes.
Dec. 17	Issue Check # 502 to Hay Manufacturing, vendor number 2, for $33,000, purchase invoice number 3533.
Dec. 20	The city council donated land with a fair market value of $5,000 to Runners Corporation as an incentive for future expansion.
Dec. 21	Issue a Check # 503 to Say Manufacturing Company, vendor number 4, for $935 in partial payment of purchase invoice number 3534.
Dec. 22	Issue Check # 504 TO All Insurance Company for $3,000. The payment represents next year's insurance coverage.

Date	Transaction
Dec. 27	Runners Corporation sold land for $4,500 cash; no gain or loss was recognized.
Dec. 28	Issue Check # 505 to Bell Advertising Agency for $4,000.
Dec. 28	Sold marketable securities for $25,000. Recognize a gain of $5,000.
Dec 30	Issue Check # 506 to US Post Office for $100. (Charge to miscellaneous expense)
Dec. 30	Issue Check # 507 to the City of Black Diamond for $350 for payment of utility bill.
Dec. 30	Purchased additional land for further plant expansion. Issue Check # 508 for $20,000 to Mary Realty.
Dec. 30	Declared and paid a special year-end 10 cents per share on the 150,000 shares of stock outstanding. Issue Check # 509.
Dec. 30	Tog Sport Shop notified us of their bankruptcy proceeding. This makes it necessary to write off their account as uncollectible.

Dec. 30	Sold merchandise on account to String Stores. The sales invoice is number 6205 and is for $1,000, terms 1/10 n/30.
	 Item Sold:
	     Item #130 – 20 pairs @ 50.00
	 Cost of Sale:
	     Item #130 – 20 pairs @ 19.95

End of Year Instructions

Monday, December 31st, is the last business day of the calendar year. You will need to proceed with the work required at the close of the annual accounting period as follows:

Using a General Journal to Enter Transactions

Ruled forms are provided for the work sheet, the schedules, and the financial statements in Appendix A.

After the transactions have been recorded in the General Journal and posted to the Ledgers, complete the following:

1. Prepare a Schedule of Accounts Receivable
2. Prepare a Schedule of Accounts Payable
1. Prepare a Trial balance before adjustments at December 31 on the ten-column work sheet.
2. Complete the ten-column work sheet as of December 31. Adjustment data needed to complete the work sheet are as follows:
    A. The physical inventory of merchandise at the close of business, December 31, 2009, showed $25,822.50.
    B. Office supplies on hand on December 31, $1,500.
    C. Insurance expired for the month of December, $250.
    D. Depreciation expense for the year 2009:
        Office equipment $8,535
        Building $7,500
    E. Management has decided to increase the Allowance for Uncollectible Accounts by $200.
    F. Accrued salaries at December 31, $7,000; do not record payroll tax accruals.
    G. Accrued interest at December 31, $400.
    H. Accrued property tax for the months of November and December, payable in April, 2009, and $1,139.
    I. Amortization of organization costs, $1,000.
    J. The income tax for 2009 is $24,000.

3. Extend the adjusted balances of the accounts to the adjusted trial balance columns of the ten-column work sheet.
4. Classify the accounts by extending the adjusted balances to the proper income statement or balance sheet columns.
5. Determine the net income for the year and enter the amount in the proper work sheet columns. Complete the work sheet by entering the totals and ruling the columns.
6. Prepare an income statement, a statement of retained earnings, a balance sheet, and statement of cash flows using the indirect method.
7. Journalize the adjusting entries in the general journal and post the accounts in the general ledger in order to bring the general ledger accounts into agreement with the financial statements.
8. Journalize the closing entries in the general journal and post the accounts to the general ledger. Indicate closed accounts by inserting a horizontal line or 0.00 in both balance columns.
9. Prepare a post-closing trial balance to prove the general ledger is in balance.

Using Special Journals to Enter Transactions

1. Total and rule each column of the various special journals. Prove equality of debits and credits in each journal.
2. Determine the cash balance at December 31st (the beginning cash balance plus the total cash receipts minus the total cash payments).
3. Post all account items that need to be posted individually to the general ledger and to the subsidiary ledgers (where appropriate).
4. Rule the journals and post the totals to the appropriate accounts in the general ledger. Determine the balance of each general ledger account.
5. Prepare schedules of accounts receivable and accounts payable and compare the totals with the respective general ledger accounts balances.
6. Prepare a trial balance before adjustments at December 31 on the ten-column work sheet. Copy the December 31 trial balance before adjustments in the first two amount columns. Ruled forms are provided for the work sheet, the schedules, and the statements. All general ledger account titles are printed on the work sheet.
7. Complete the ten-column work sheet as of December 31. Adjustment data needed to complete the work sheet are as follows:
   A. The physical inventory of merchandise at the close of business, December 31, 2009, showed $25,822.50.
   B. Office supplies on hand on December 31, $1,500.
   C. Insurance expired for the month of December, $250.
   D. Depreciation expense for the year 2009:
   Office equipment $8,535
   Building $7,500
   E. Management has decided to increase the allowance account by $200.
   F. Accrued salaries at December 31, $7,000; do not record payroll tax accruals.
   G. Accrued interest at December 31, $400.
   H. Accrued property tax for the months of November and December, payable in April, 2009, and $1,139.
   I. Amortization of organization costs, $1,000.
   J. The income tax for 2009 is $24,000.
10. Extend the adjusted balances of the accounts to the adjusted trial balance columns of the ten-column work sheet.
11. Classify the accounts by extending the adjusted balances to the proper income statement or balance sheet columns.
12. Determine the net income for the year and enter the amount in the proper work sheet columns. Complete the work sheet by entering the totals and ruling the columns.
13. Prepare an income statement, a statement of retained earnings, a balance sheet, and statement of cash flows using the indirect method.
14. Journalize the adjusting entries in the general journal and post the accounts in the general ledger in order to bring the general ledger accounts into agreement with the financial statements.

15. Journalize the closing entries in the general journal and post the accounts to the general ledger. Indicate closed accounts by inserting a horizontal line or 0.00 in both balance columns.
16. Prepare a post-closing trial balance to prove the general ledger is in balance.

CHAPTER 3

PH General Ledger Software

In this chapter, you will begin installing the Prentice Hall General Ledger Software with data files for Runners Corporation. Then you will record the transactions for December in the journal, post to the ledger, and view and print the appropriate reports. To become familiar with the PH General Ledger environment, refer to Appendices B, C, and D.

Installation of PH General Ledger Software

This section discusses several basic operations that you need to complete to install PH General Ledger program and the student data file for use in completing the computer workshop assignment. PH General Ledger Software has **Help Content** as well as a **Quick Tour** to become familiar with the features of the program. Refer to Appendix B to become familiar with the PH General Ledger Software desktop environment.

System Requirements

The recommended minimum software and hardware requirements your computer system needs to run both Windows and PH General Ledger Software successfully are:

- PH General Ledger Software for Microsoft Windows. The program comes on one CD.
- IBM Compatible 350 MHz Pentium II or higher processor
- Windows 2000 or XP
- A minimum of 128 MB of RAM (memory) with 256 MB RAM recommended
- A video card that will support at least 256 colors.
- Video resolution of at least 800 x 600 pixels (1024 x 768 or higher recommended.
- Internet Explorer
- Printers supported by Windows XP/2000
- CD-Rom Drive
- Online features require Internet access. Minimum connection speed depends on service
- Mouse or compatible pointing device

CD-ROM CONTENTS

The PH General Ledger Software installation and program files (in condensed form), Runners Corporation, and A-1 Photography data files for use in completing the practice set are on the CD-ROM that accompanies this text.

Installation Procedure: PH General Ledger Software

To install PH General Ledger Software on your computer, follow these instructions. Installing data files is a secondary procedure, and follows:

1. Start Windows.
2. Make sure that no other programs are running on your system.
3. Insert the CD-ROM in your CD-ROM drive.
4. Click on the Start button; then click on Run.
5. Type d:\start.exe and press the ENTER key, where "d" stands for the letter of your computer's CD-ROM drive.
6. From the CD's opening screen, click on the Install button.
7. Select **Prentice Hall General Ledger**, and then follow the step-by-step installation instructions as they appear on the screen.
8. When installation is complete, you may see a message informing you to restart your system. Complete the installation of the data files before restarting (see below).

Installation Procedures: Data Files

1. From the CD's Install screen, select **Prentice Hall General Ledger - Data files**.
2. The file will extract to the directory C:\Program Files\Prentice Hall\Practice Sets 2009 on your computer. To do this, click the Unzip button on the WinZip Self-Extractor, and then click Close.
3. Put your CD-ROM away for safekeeping
4. Exit the CD.
5. *Restart your computer so the General Ledger program can work properly.* (This may take a while.)
6. After restarting your computer, open General Ledger. After logging into the program, practice set data files can be found by choosing File > Open, and navigating to the directory where the files were placed (C:\Program Files\Prentice Hall\Practice Sets 2009).

Using PH General Ledger Software on a Network

PH General Ledger Software can be used in a network environment as long as each student uses a separate Student Data File source to store his or her data file. Students should consult with their instructor and/or network administrator for specific procedures regarding program installation and any special printing procedures required for proper network operation.

Student Data File Integrity

PH General Ledger Software will run most efficiently if the Runners Corporation data file is installed on a hard drive. This can be on the internal or an external hard drive or in a unique student folder on a network drive. Use of an external USB drive enables you to take your file with you. Check with your professor on the storage location of your data.

Opening Runners Corporation and PH General Ledger Data Files

1. Click on the **Start** button on the taskbar. Point to All Programs, point to **Prentice Hall**, point to **PH General Ledger v5**, and then click **PH General Ledger v5**.

2. The Logon Screen displays. Enter your name, school identification number and the class section number.

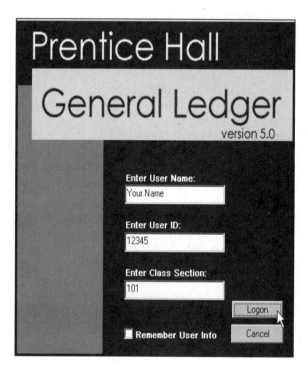

3. Click **Logon**. The opening Window displays.

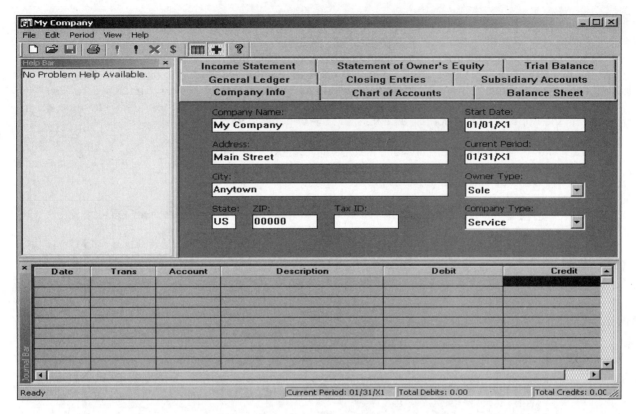

4. From the PH General Ledger Software menu bar, click **File** and click **Open**. The PH General Ledger open dialog box displays. Double-click **Practice Sets 2009**.

5. The Open dialog box displays. Select **Runners Corporation** and click **Open**. The company name appears in the title bar and the company information window displays.

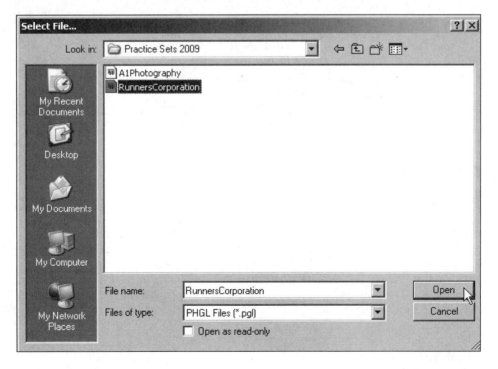

Displaying Trial Balance, General Ledger, Subsidiary Ledgers

It is important for you to be able to identify the specific reports that you print for each assignment as your own, particularly if you are using a computer that shares a printer with other computers. PH General Ledger Software prints the name of the company you are working with at the top of each report. To personalize your reports so that you can identify the company and your printed reports, your name will display in the upper left hand corner, as entered in the Logon window.

Under the standard toolbar, there are tabs that identify different information.

1. Click the Chart of Accounts tab to display the chart.

Number	Name	Account Type	Balance Type	Beginning Balance
10100	Cash	Current Asset	Normal Debit	56,386.00
10500	Marketable Securities	Current Asset	Normal Debit	20,000.00
11000	Accounts Receivable	Accounts Receivable	Normal Debit	47,839.00
11100	Allowance for Uncollectible A	Current Asset	Normal Credit	4,500.00
11500	Inventory	Current Asset	Normal Debit	20,595.00
11700	Prepaid Insurance	Current Asset	Normal Debit	250.00
11900	Office Supplies	Current Asset	Normal Debit	2,000.00
16000	Land	Plant & Equipment	Normal Debit	10,000.00
17000	Building	Plant & Equipment	Normal Debit	150,000.00
17500	Accumulated Depreciation-B	Plant & Equipment	Normal Credit	7,500.00
18000	Office Equipment	Plant & Equipment	Normal Debit	42,675.00
18500	Accumulated Depreciation-C	Plant & Equipment	Normal Credit	8,535.00
19000	Organization Costs	Other Asset	Normal Debit	5,000.00
20100	Accounts Payable	Accounts Payable	Normal Credit	56,803.00
20200	Income Tax Payable	Current Liability	Normal Credit	.00
20300	Salaries Payable	Current Liability	Normal Credit	.00
20400	Cash Dividends Payable	Current Liability	Normal Credit	.00
20500	Interest Payable	Current Liability	Normal Credit	.00
20600	Note Payable	Current Liability	Normal Credit	.00
20700	Property Tax Payable	Current Liability	Normal Credit	.00
30100	Common Stock	Equity	Normal Credit	100,000.00
30200	Premium on Common Stock	Equity	Normal Credit	.00
35000	Retained Earnings	Retained Earnings	Normal Credit	68,662.00
36000	Donated Capital	Equity	Normal Credit	.00
41000	Sales	Revenue	Normal Credit	475,445.00
41500	Sales Discounts	Revenue	Normal Debit	4,000.00
41600	Sales Returns and Allowanc	Revenue	Normal Debit	2,000.00
51000	Cost of Goods Sold	Cost Of Goods Sold	Normal Debit	206,000.00
60100	Salaries Expense	Expenses	Normal Debit	133,685.00
60200	Utilities Expense	Expenses	Normal Debit	3,000.00
60300	Office Supplies Expense	Expenses	Normal Debit	2,000.00
60400	Advertisement Expense	Expenses	Normal Debit	7,000.00
60500	Depreciation Expense-Office	Expenses	Normal Debit	.00
60600	Depreciation Expense-Buildi	Expenses	Normal Debit	.00
60700	Insurance Expense	Expenses	Normal Debit	2,750.00
60800	Uncollectible Accounts Expe	Expenses	Normal Debit	4,500.00
60900	Property Tax Expense	Expenses	Normal Debit	1,665.00
61000	Miscellaneous Expense	Expenses	Normal Debit	100.00
61100	Gain on Sale of Marketable !	Expenses	Normal Debit	.00
61200	Interest Expense	Expenses	Normal Debit	.00
61300	Amortization of Organization	Expenses	Normal Debit	.00
61400	Income Tax	Expenses	Normal Debit	.00

2. Click the General Ledger tab to display the ledger accounts. Verify the balances by comparing the amounts shown in the General Ledger with the amounts shown in the Trial Balance on page 2.
3. Click the Trial Balance tab to display the trial balance as it appears on the next page.
   (Note regarding the following reports: each report's heading includes your name in the upper left corner of the page and the date and time prepared in the upper right corner of the page. Your report will show your computer's current date and time and may be different than the examples given.)

```
Your Name                    Runners Corporation              12/01/2009 15:27
                               Trial Balance
                                 12/31/X9
```

Account	Debit	Credit
Cash	56386.00	
Marketable Securities	20000.00	
Accounts Receivable	47839.00	
Allowance for Uncollectible Accounts		4500.00
Inventory	20595.00	
Prepaid Insurance	250.00	
Office Supplies	2000.00	
Land	10000.00	
Building	150000.00	
Accumulated Depreciation-Building		7500.00
Office Equipment	42675.00	
Accumulated Depreciation-Office Equipment		8535.00
Organization Costs	5000.00	
Accounts Payable		56803.00
Income Tax Payable		0.00
Salaries Payable		0.00
Cash Dividends Payable		0.00
Interest Payable		0.00
Note Payable		0.00
Property Tax Payable		0.00
Common Stock		100000.00
Premium on Common Stock		0.00
Retained Earnings		68662.00
Donated Capital		0.00
Sales		475445.00
Sales Discounts	4000.00	
Sales Returns and Allowances	2000.00	
Cost of Goods Sold	206000.00	
Salaries Expense	133685.00	
Utilities Expense	3000.00	
Office Supplies Expense	2000.00	
Advertisement Expense	7000.00	
Depreciation Expense-Office Equipment	0.00	
Depreciation Expense-Building	0.00	
Insurance Expense	2750.00	
Uncollectible Accounts Expense	4500.00	
Property Tax Expense	1665.00	
Miscellaneous Expense	100.00	
Gain on Sale of Marketable Securities	0.00	
Interest Expense	0.00	
Amortization of Organization Costs	0.00	
Income Tax	0.00	
TOTALS	721445.00	721445.00

4. Click the **Subsidiary Accounts** tab to display the Accounts Receivable and Accounts Payable ledgers. Click the **Details** button. Select **Accounts Receivable** from the drop-down list. The Customer Accounts appear below:

```
Your Name                    Runners Corporation              12/01/2009 15:30
                             Subsidiary Accounts
                             12/31/X9
_____


Accounts Receivable :
Active Sporting Stores - Beginning                                    28689.00
Active Sporting Stores - Current                                      28689.00

All Sporting - Beginning                                              4000.00
All Sporting - Current                                                4000.00

Home Shoes Center - Beginning                                        13150.00
Home Shoes Center - Current                                          13150.00

String Stores - Beginning                                               0.00
String Stores - Current                                                 0.00

Tog Sport Shop - Beginning                                           2000.00
Tog Sport Shop - Current                                             2000.00

True Sports Shop - Beginning                                            0.00
True Sports Shop - Current                                              0.00

Total AR Subsidiaries                                               47839.00
```

5. Click the **Subsidiary Accounts** tab to display the Accounts Receivable and Accounts Payable ledgers. Click the **Details** button. Select **Accounts Payable** from the drop-down list. The Vendor Accounts appear below:

```
Your Name                    Runners Corporation              12/01/2009 15:32
                             Subsidiary Accounts
                             12/31/X9
_____


Accounts Payable :
Hay Manufacturing Company - Beginning                               33000.00
Hay Manufacturing Company - Current                                 33000.00

Hoot Manufacturing Company - Beginning                              18000.00
Hoot Manufacturing Company - Current                                18000.00

Say Manufacturing Company - Beginning                                5803.00
Say Manufacturing Company - Current                                  5803.00

Tic Manufacturing Company - Beginning                                   0.00
Tic Manufacturing Company - Current                                     0.00

Tice Manufacturing Company - Beginning                                  0.00
Tice Manufacturing Company - Current                                    0.00

Total AP Subsidiaries                                               56803.00
```

Computerizing Runners Corporation

The business transactions for Runners Corporation are displayed on the following pages. The PH General Ledger Software should be open with Runners Corporation displaying on the title bar. The main window should display:

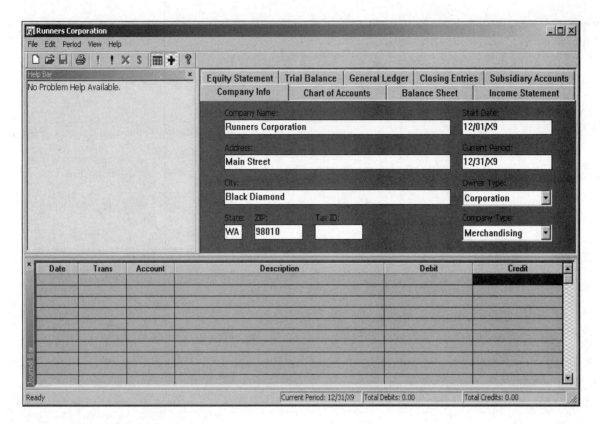

Entering Transactions

Below are the December 2009 transactions for Runners Corporation. The date, transaction description and instruction are listed. The instruction column will direct you to record each transaction in the general journal. Occasionally, there will be screen shots placed within the transactions to show you how your screen should look. Click the **Save** icon 💾

Date	Transaction	Instruction
Dec. 1	Received a check no. 202 from Active Sporting Stores, customer number 2052, for $28,689 in full settlement of the account. **Note** when you click in the Date, Account or Description columns, a down arrow will appear. Click it and make a selection. By contrast, the Debit and Credit columns require dollar amounts to be entered.	Record using the **General Journal**. Click in the Date column, click the down arrow and select 12/01/X9. Notice the transaction number automatically displays. Click in the Account column, click the down arrow and select Cash. Notice the account description automatically displays. Click in the Debit column and enter 28689. Click in the Account column on the next line and select Accounts Receivable Active Sporting Stores. Click in the Credit column and enter 28689. Enter the journal entry description, "Received cash on account" in the drop down box area under the description column. The journal entry displays.

Date	Transaction	Instruction

Screen Shot

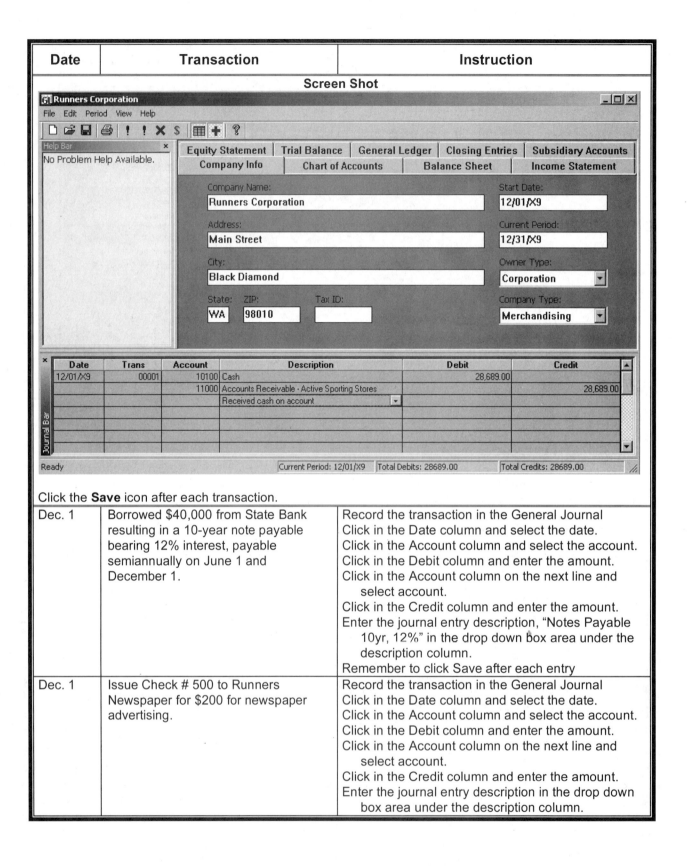

Click the **Save** icon after each transaction.

Date	Transaction	Instruction
Dec. 1	Borrowed $40,000 from State Bank resulting in a 10-year note payable bearing 12% interest, payable semiannually on June 1 and December 1.	Record the transaction in the General Journal Click in the Date column and select the date. Click in the Account column and select the account. Click in the Debit column and enter the amount. Click in the Account column on the next line and select account. Click in the Credit column and enter the amount. Enter the journal entry description, "Notes Payable 10yr, 12%" in the drop down box area under the description column. Remember to click Save after each entry
Dec. 1	Issue Check # 500 to Runners Newspaper for $200 for newspaper advertising.	Record the transaction in the General Journal Click in the Date column and select the date. Click in the Account column and select the account. Click in the Debit column and enter the amount. Click in the Account column on the next line and select account. Click in the Credit column and enter the amount. Enter the journal entry description in the drop down box area under the description column.

Date	Transaction	Instruction

Dec. 2	Sold merchandise on account to String Stores, customer number 2058. The sales invoice is number 6202 and is for $4,000, terms 1/10 n/30. Runners Corporation uses a perpetual inventory system and therefore records the cost of merchandise sold as well as the sale.
	Items sold:
	    Item # 105 – 40 pairs @ 75.00
	    Item # 130 – 20 pairs @ 50.00
	Cost of Sale:
	    Item # 105 – 40 pairs @ 25.00
	    Item # 130 – 20 pairs @ 19.95
		Record using the **General Journal**. For a sale on account, a journal entry must be made for the retail sale as well as for the cost of the sale.
		Click in the **Date** column and select **12/02/X9**.
		Click in the Account column and select Accounts Receivable - String Stores.
		Click in the Debit column and enter the amount 4,000.
		Click in the Description column and select Sales.
		Click in the Credit column and enter the amount 4,000.
		Enter the journal entry description, "Sold Merchandise on Account" in the drop down box area under the description column.
		Click in the Date column and select 12/02/X9.
		Click in the Account column and select Cost of Goods Sold.
		Click in the Debit column and enter the amount (Calculate the amount by multiplying the Cost of Sale quantity by the Cost of Sale price. For example, 40 x 25 = 1000 and 20 x 19.95 = 399. Add the two amounts together to get the total.).
		Click in Account column and select the Inventory account.
		Click in the Credit column and enter the amount.
		Enter the journal entry description, "Cost of sale" in the drop down area under the description column.
		The journal displays below.

Screen Shot

Date	Trans	Account	Description	Debit	Credit
12/02/X9	00004	11000	Accounts Receivable - String Stores	4,000.00	
		41000	Sales		4,000.00
			Sold Merchandise on Account		
12/02/X9	00005	51000	Cost of Goods Sold	1,399.00	
		11500	Inventory		1,399.00
			Cost of Sale		

Ready   Current Period: 12/02/X9   Total Debits: 74288.00   Total Credits: 74288.00

Date	Transaction	Instruction
Dec. 2	Purchased merchandise on account from Tice Manufacturing Company, Vendor Number 1. The purchase invoice is number 3356 for $8,464, terms net 30. Items purchased: Item #130—400 pairs @ 19.95 Item #120 – 22 pairs @ 22.00	Record using the General Journal. Click in the Date column and select 12/02/X9. Click in the Account column and select Inventory. Click in the Debit column and enter the amount. Click in the Account column and select Accounts Payable - Tice Manufacturing Company. Click in the Credit column and enter the amount. Enter the journal entry description, "Purchased on account net 30" in the drop down box area under the description column. The journal entry is:

Date	Transaction	Instruction

| | | Screen Shot |

Date	Trans	Account	Description	Debit	Credit
12/02/X9	00006	11500	Inventory	8,464.00	
		20100	Accounts Payable - Tice Manufacturing Company		8,464.00
			Purchased on account, Net 30		

Date	Transaction	Instruction
Dec 3	Sold merchandise on account; invoice number 6203, to True Sports Shop, customer number 2055, for $30,000. Terms of the sale were 1/10 n/30. Items sold: Item #130 – 200 pairs @ 50.00 Item #120 – 100 pairs @ 65.00 Item #110 – 150 pairs @ 90.00 Cost of Sale: Item #130 – 200 pairs @ 19.95 Item #120 – 100 pairs @ 22.00 Item #110 – 150 pairs @ 35.00	Record the retail sale and cost of sale using the example for the December 2nd transaction above.
Dec. 6	Sold merchandise to S.T. Sporting for cash, $18,500, check no. 481. Items sold: Item #105 – 100 pairs @ 75.00 Item #110 – 50 pairs @ 90.00 Item #120 – 100 pairs @65.00 Cost of Sale: Item #105 – 100 pairs @25.00 Item #110 – 50 pairs @ 35.00 Item #120 – 100 pairs @ 22.00	Record the retail sale and cost of sale.
Dec. 8	Sold merchandise to North Shoes, located at 105 NE 8th, Bellevue, WA 98009, customer number 2062, for $2,500. The sales invoice number is 6204. Terms 1/10 n/30. Item sold: Item #130 – 50 pairs @ 50.00 Cost of Sale: Item #130 – 50 pairs @ 19.95	To add a customer: Click the Subsidiary Accounts tab. Click Add. The wizard displays. Click Next. Enter North Shoes and select Accounts Receivable from the Account Type drop- down list. Click Next. Click Finish. Click in the General Journal and enter the transaction. Record the retail sale and cost of sale.

Date	Transaction	Instruction
Dec. 8	Received a check no. 255 from All Sporting, customer number 2056, for $4,000 in payment of invoice number 6192.	Record the transaction in the General Journal Click in the Date column and select the date. Click in the Account column and select the account. Click in the Debit column and enter the amount. Click in the Account column on the next line and select the credit account. Click in the Credit column and enter the amount. Enter the journal entry description in the drop down box area under the description column.
Dec. 9	Received a check no. 898 from String Stores, customer number 2058, for $3,960. The invoice number is 6202, and a sales discount of $40 was taken.	Record the transaction in the General Journal. Be sure to record the sales discount.
Dec. 9	Purchased merchandise from Tic Manufacturing Company, vendor number 5. The purchase invoice is number 3538 for $23,350. Terms 30 days. Items purchased: Item #105 – 400 pairs @ 25.00 Item #110 – 350 pairs @ 35.00 Item #120 – 50 pairs @ 22.00	Record the transaction in the General Journal as shown in the December 2nd transaction.
Dec. 9	Returned $1,300 worth of merchandise to Say Manufacturing Company, vendor 4. Received a credit memorandum acknowledging a reduction in the liability account of $1,300. Item returned: Item #105 – 52 pairs @ 25.00	Record using the General Journal. Be sure to reduce Say Manufacturing Company account.
Dec 10	Received a check no. 305 from True Sports Shop, customer number 2055, for $29,700 in payment of invoice number 6203, sales discount $300.	Record using the General Journal.
Dec. 10	Sold merchandise to Hale Sporting Goods for cash (check no. 442), $9,750. Items sold: Item #105—130 pairs @ 75.00 Cost of Sale: Item #105—130 pairs @ 25.00	Record the retail sale and cost of sale.
Dec. 13	Issue Check # 501 to Hoot Manufacturing, vendor number 3, for $18,000 in payment of purchase invoice number 3532.	Record using the General Journal.
Dec. 14	Received $70,000 for the sale of 50,000 shares of $1 par value common stock.	Record using the General Journal.
Dec. 15	Received a check no. 678 from North Shoes, customer number 2062, for $2,475, invoice number 6204. A sales discount of $25 was taken by North Shoes.	Record using the General Journal. Be sure to record the sales discount.

Date	Transaction	Instruction
Dec. 17	Issue Check # 502 to Hay Manufacturing Company, vendor number 2, for $33,000, purchase invoice number 3533.	Record using the General Journal.
Dec. 20	The city council donated land with a fair market value of $5,000 to Runners Corporation as an incentive for future expansion.	Record using the General Journal.
Dec. 21	Issue a Check # 503 to Say Manufacturing Company, vendor number 4, for $935 in partial payment of purchase invoice number 3534.	Record using the General Journal.
Dec. 22	Issue Check # 504 TO All Insurance Company for $3,000. The payment represents next year's insurance coverage.	Record using the General Journal.
Dec. 27	Runners Corporation sold land for $4,500 cash; no gain or loss was recognized.	Record using the General Journal.
Dec. 28	Issue Check # 505 to Bell Advertising Agency for $4,000.	Record using the General Journal.
Dec. 28	Sold marketable securities for $25,000. Recognize a gain of $5,000.	Record using the General Journal.
Dec 30	Issue Check # 506 to US Post Office for $100. (Charge to miscellaneous expense)	Record using the General Journal.
Dec. 30	Issue Check # 507 to the City of Black Diamond for $350 for payment of utility bill.	Record using the General Journal.
Dec. 30	Purchased additional land for further plant expansion. Issue Check # 508 for $20,000 to Mary Realty.	Record using the General Journal.
Dec. 30	Declared and paid a special year-end 10 cents per share on the 150,000 shares of stock outstanding. Issue Check # 509.	Record using the General Journal.
Dec. 30	Tog Sport Shop notified us of their bankruptcy proceeding. This makes it necessary to write off their account as uncollectible.	Record using the General Journal.
Dec. 30	Sold merchandise on account to String Stores. The sales invoice is number 6205 and is for $1,000, terms 1/10 n/30. Items sold: Item #130 – 20 pairs @ 50.00 Cost of Sale: Item #130 – 20 pairs @ 19.95	Record the retail sale and cost of sale.

Date	Transaction	Instruction
	After completing all transactions, **Post** the transactions to the ledger.	Review all transactions before posting. After reviewing all transactions: Click the Post button (blue exclamation point) from the standard tool bar. Click Yes. Click OK to complete the process. Note after posting the transactions turn blue in color. Click Save
	BACKUP DATA files before entering adjusting entries.	Click File from menu bar. Click Save As. Enter the file name Runners Corporation Before Adjustments Click Save

End of Year Instructions

Thursday, December 31st, is the last business day of the calendar year. You will need to proceed with the work required at the close of the annual accounting period as follows:

Printing Reports before Adjustments

Name of Report	Instruction	Check Figures
Any Report	Click **File** on menu bar. Click **Print**. Select the reports to print. Click **Print**.	
General Ledger	Click the General Ledger tab.	Cash Balance is $198,375.00
Trial Balance	Click the Trial Balance tab.	$868,774.00

Entering Adjusting Entries

Enter the following adjusting entries using the General Journal.

1. The physical inventory of merchandise at the close of business, December 31, 2009, showed $25,822.50. Be sure to refer to the Trial Balance to verify adjustment accounts.
2. Office supplies on hand on December 31, $1,500.
3. Insurance expired for the month of December, $250.
4. Depreciation expense for the year 2009: (You can enter a compound entry)
       Office equipment $8,535
       Building $7,500
5. Management has decided to increase the uncollectible allowance account by $200.
6. Accrued salaries at December 31, $7,000; do not record payroll tax accruals.
7. Accrued interest at December 31, $400.
8. Accrued property tax for the months of November and December, payable in April, 2009, $1,139.
9. Amortization of organization costs, $1,000.
10. The income tax for 2009 is $24,000.

After completing all adjusting entries transactions, Post the transactions to the ledger. Review all transactions before posting. After reviewing all transactions:

- Click the **Post** button (blue exclamation point) from the standard tool bar.
- Click **Yes**.
- Click **OK** to complete the process.
- Click **Save** to save the file

Note after posting the transactions turn blue in color.

Printing Reports for Year End

Name of Report	Instructions	Check Figures
Any Report	Click **File** on menu bar Click **Print** Select the reports to print Click **Print**	
General Ledger	Click the General Ledger tab	Cash Balance $198,375.00
Trial Balance	Click the Trial Balance tab	$917,548.00
Income Statement	Click the Income Statement tab	$98,669.50
Retained Earnings	Click the Statement of Equity tab	$152,331.50
Balance Sheet	Click the Balance Sheet tab	$435,252.50
Accounts Receivable	Click the Subsidiary Accounts tab Click Details Click the drop-down box and select Accounts Receivable	$14,150.00
Accounts Payable	Click Subsidiary Accounts tab Click Details Click the drop-down box and select Accounts Payable	$35,382.00

If all balances are correct, then refer to **Appendix D** to backup your data files. If not review the General Journal and correct any transactions using instructions in **Appendix C**.

Closing a Period

In a manual accounting system a Post-Closing Trial Balance is created to verify the closing process and to prove the equality of debits and credits. PH General Ledger has an automated close process displaying the closing entries for your review. Click the **Close** button (red exclamation point) from the standard tool bar. Click **OK** twice to complete the closing process. Click the Closing Entries tab to display the closing entries. After performing the closing process backup the company data files.

Runners Corporation

Chapter 4

QuickBooks Pro 2008 or 2009 Software

In this chapter, you will begin installing the QuickBooks Pro 2008 or 2009 Data Files for Runners Corporation. Then, you will record the transactions for December using the Company, Customer & Sales, Vendor & Purchases, and Banking Centers. To become familiar with the QuickBooks Pro 2008 or 2009 environment, refer to Appendices B, C, and D.

The Runners Corporation data file used in completing the practice set is on the CD-ROM that accompanies this text.

Installation Procedure: QuickBooks Pro 2008 or 2009 Data Files for Runners Corporation

To place the Runners Corporation Practice Set data file for use with QuickBooks Pro onto your computer's hard disk, follow these instructions:

1. Start Windows.
2. Make sure that no other programs are running on your system.
3. Insert the CD-ROM into your CD-ROM drive.
4. Click on the Start button; then click on Run.
5. Type d:\start.exe and press the ENTER key, where "d" stands for the letter of your computer's CD-ROM drive.
6. From the CD's opening screen, click on Install CD Content.
7. From the Install screen, click on **QuickBooks Pro Practice Sets.**
8. Click the Unzip button on the WinZip Self-Extractor
9. Files will extract to C:\QuickBooks2009 on your computer. Change this default directory designation to your designated hard drive location/Practice Sets-QuickBooks
10. When finished, put your CD-ROM away for safekeeping
11. Exit the CD

Using QuickBooks Pro 2008 or 2009 on a Network

QuickBooks can be used in a network environment as long as each student uses a separate Student Data File source to store his or her data file. Students should consult with their instructor and/or network administrator for specific procedures regarding program installation and any special printing procedures required for proper network operation.

Student Data File Integrity

QuickBooks Pro 2008 or 2009 can use the Runners Corporation data file on a hard drive, a network drive, or a USB drive.

Opening QuickBooks Pro 2008 or 2009 Data Files for Runners Corporation

1. Click on the **Start** button. Point to **Programs**; point to the QuickBooks Pro folder and select **QuickBooks Pro 2008 or 2009**. Your desktop may have the QuickBooks icon allowing for a quicker entrance into the program by double clicking it.
2. From the **File** menu, click **Open Company or Restore Company**.
3. Click **Open a company file**, click **Next** on the Open or Restore Company dialog box

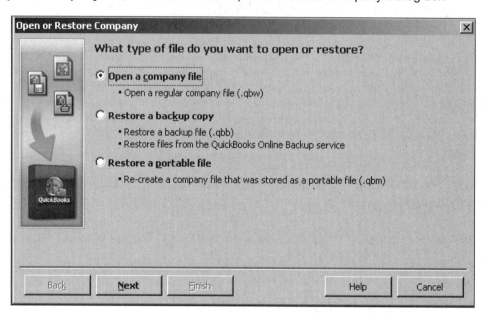

4. Click the drop-down arrow for **Look in:** and select the location where you saved Runners Corporation. Click the company file name **Runners Corporation**, then click **Open**.

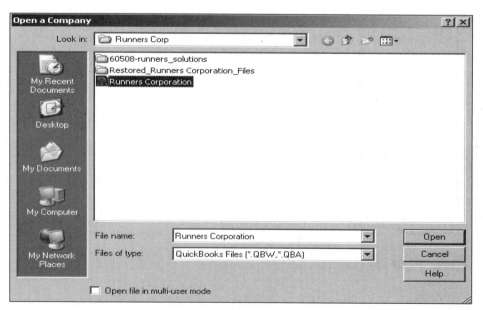

The QuickBooks Pro opening work area displays. Runners Corporation appears in the title bar of the main window.

Customize the Company Name

QuickBooks Pro 2008 or 2009 prints the name of the company you are working with at the top of each report. To personalize your reports so that you can identify both the company and your printed reports, the company name needs to be modified.

1. Click the **Company** menu. Click **Company Information**. The program will respond by bringing up a dialog box allowing the user to edit/add information about the company.
2. Click in the **Company Name** entry field at the end of **Runners Corporation**. If it is already highlighted, press the right arrow key.
3. Add a dash and your real name or initials to the end of the company name. Your screen will look similar to the one shown below: When finished, click **OK**.

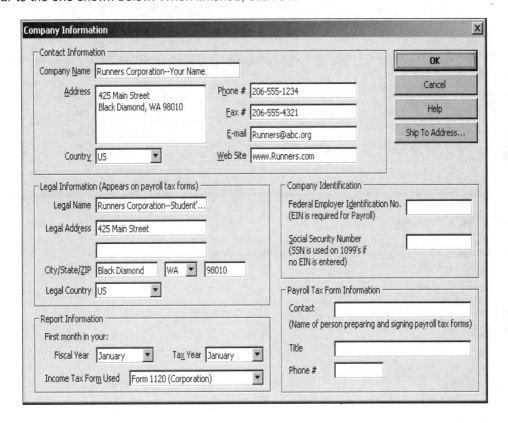

Displaying Reports Using the Report Center

Reports give you information about your company and the transactions you enter. While you may prepare reports in various areas in QuickBooks, all of the reports available may be prepared in the Report Center.

Open the Report Center

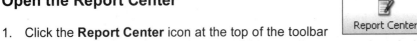

1. Click the **Report Center** icon at the top of the toolbar
2. The Report Center shows different categories of reports on the left side of the screen and individual report names within a category and their descriptions on the right side of the screen.

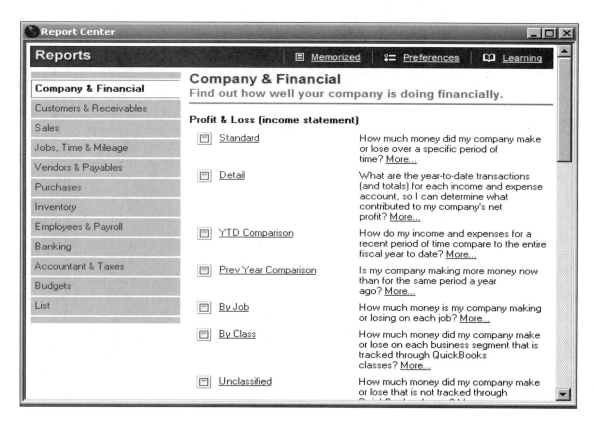

Trial Balance

1. Click **Accountant & Taxes** on the left of the Report Center
2. Click **Trial Balance**.
3. Tab to the From field and enter **12/01/09**.
4. Tab to the To field and enter **12/01/09**.
5. Press Tab and the Trial Balance will display. Verify the balances.

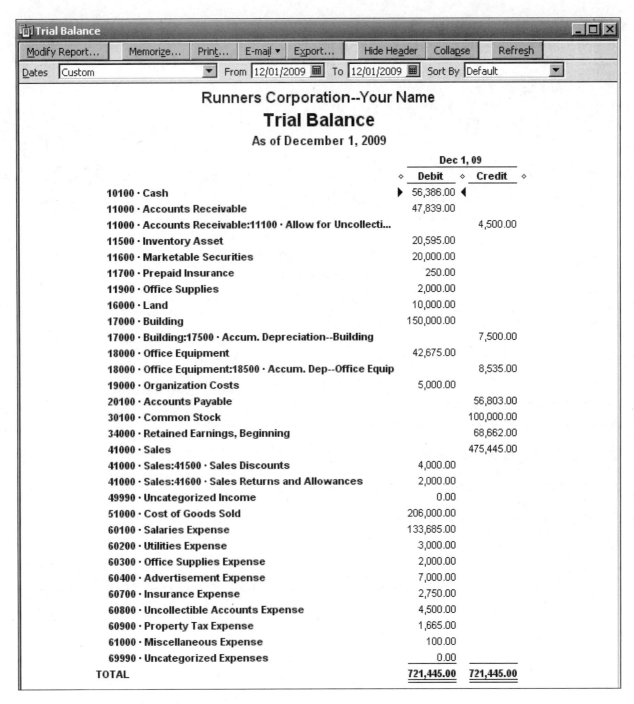

Runners Corporation--Your Name

Trial Balance

As of December 1, 2009

	Dec 1, 09	
	Debit	Credit
10100 · Cash	56,386.00	
11000 · Accounts Receivable	47,839.00	
11000 · Accounts Receivable:11100 · Allow for Uncollecti...		4,500.00
11500 · Inventory Asset	20,595.00	
11600 · Marketable Securities	20,000.00	
11700 · Prepaid Insurance	250.00	
11900 · Office Supplies	2,000.00	
16000 · Land	10,000.00	
17000 · Building	150,000.00	
17000 · Building:17500 · Accum. Depreciation--Building		7,500.00
18000 · Office Equipment	42,675.00	
18000 · Office Equipment:18500 · Accum. Dep--Office Equip		8,535.00
19000 · Organization Costs	5,000.00	
20100 · Accounts Payable		56,803.00
30100 · Common Stock		100,000.00
34000 · Retained Earnings, Beginning		68,662.00
41000 · Sales		475,445.00
41000 · Sales:41500 · Sales Discounts	4,000.00	
41000 · Sales:41600 · Sales Returns and Allowances	2,000.00	
49990 · Uncategorized Income	0.00	
51000 · Cost of Goods Sold	206,000.00	
60100 · Salaries Expense	133,685.00	
60200 · Utilities Expense	3,000.00	
60300 · Office Supplies Expense	2,000.00	
60400 · Advertisement Expense	7,000.00	
60700 · Insurance Expense	2,750.00	
60800 · Uncollectible Accounts Expense	4,500.00	
60900 · Property Tax Expense	1,665.00	
61000 · Miscellaneous Expense	100.00	
69990 · Uncategorized Expenses	0.00	
TOTAL	**721,445.00**	**721,445.00**

6. Close the window. A message displays asking if you would like to add this report to the Memorized Report list. Click **No**

General Ledger

1. In the Accountant and Taxes section of the Report Center, click **General Ledger**.
2. Tab to the From field and enter **12/01/09**.
3. Tab to the To field and enter **12/01/09**.
4. Press Tab and the General Ledger accounts will display.
5. View the balances shown for each account.
6. Close the window. Do not add the report to the Memorized Report list.

Accounts Receivable Aging Summary

1. Click **Customers and Receivables** in the Report center.
2. Click **A/R Aging Summary**.
3. Tab to the date field and enter **12/01/09**.
4. Click in the report area.
5. The customer names, balances, and aging appear. The Allowance Account balance is also shown.

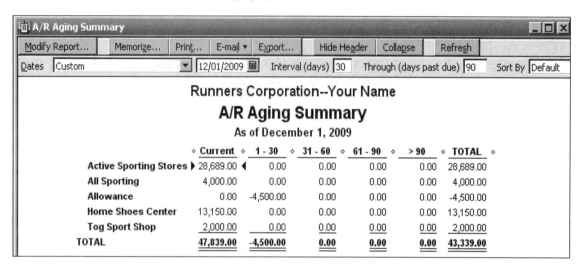

6. Close the window. Do not add the report to the Memorized Report list.

Accounts Payable Summary

1. Click **Vendors & Payables** in the Report Center
2. Click **A/P Aging Summary**.
3. Tab to the date field and enter **12/01/09**.
4. Click in the report area.
5. The vendor names, total amounts owed and aging is displayed.

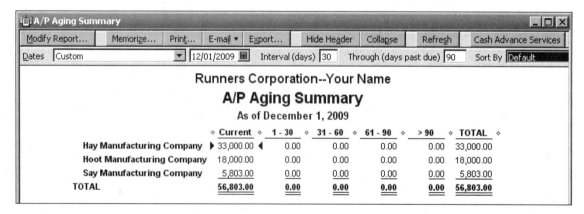

6. Close the window. A message displays asking if you would like to add this report to the Memorized Report list. Click Yes and click OK to accept the name of the report.

Any of these reports can be printed by clicking the **Print** button from the menu bar of the displayed report. Note each report's heading includes your name.

Computerizing Runners Corporation

The business transactions for Runners Corporation are displayed on the following pages. QuickBooks Pro 2008 or 2009 should be open with Runners Corporation—Your Name displaying on the title bar. The main window should display as shown below. If the icons for Vendors and Customers are not displayed, click the **Home** button on the toolbar.

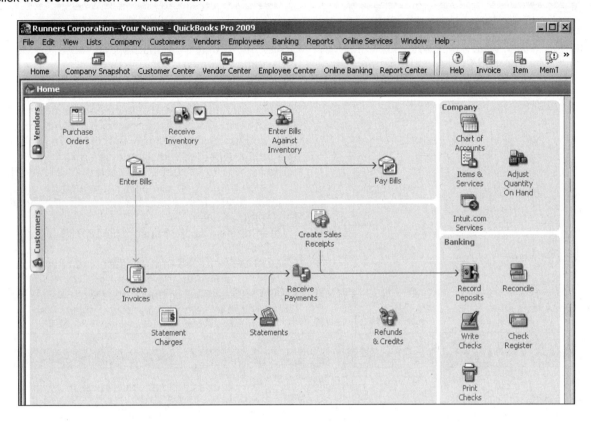

Entering Transactions

Below are the December 2009 transactions for Runners Corporation. The date, transaction description and instructions are listed. The instruction column will direct you to record each transaction. Occasionally, there will be screen shots placed within the transactions to show you how your screen should look.

Date	Transaction	Instruction
Dec. 1	Received a check no. 202 from Active Sporting Stores, customer number 2052, for $28,689 in full settlement of the account.	Click the **Receive Payments** icon shown on the Home Page Click No or Cancel to the Merchant Credit Card Account Message box or to launching a Web browser. (This may display the first time.) Click the drop-down list arrow for Received From. Click Active Sporting Stores and press Tab. Enter amount received and press Tab. The invoice for 11/30/09 is selected. (If the invoice is listed below, you can also place a check mark before the invoice and the amount will appear automatically.) Enter the date of the transaction **12/01/09,** press Tab. Select check as the Pmt. Method and press Tab. Enter the check number and press Tab. Enter "Paid in Full" in the memo field. The Receive Payments window displays with the payment information entered.

Screen Shot

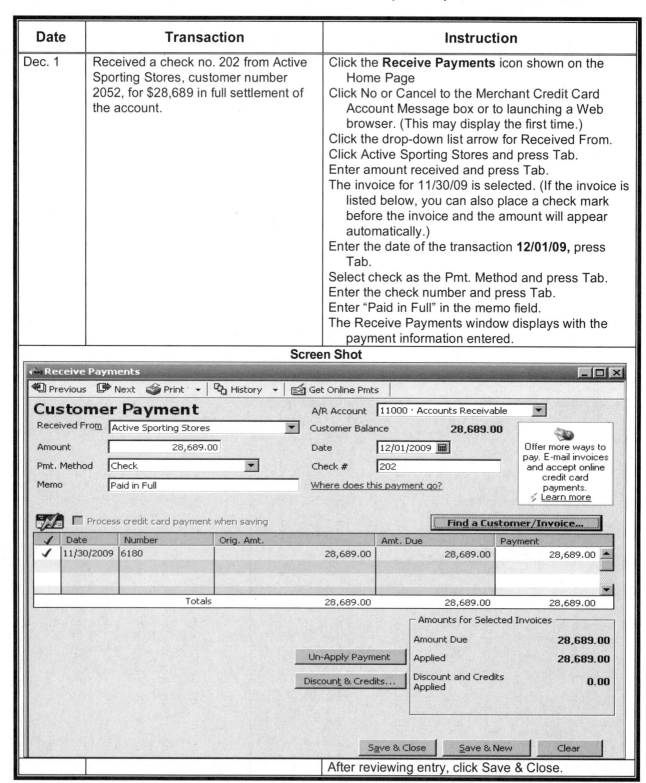

		After reviewing entry, click Save & Close.

Date	Transaction	Instruction
Dec. 1	Borrowed $40,000 from State Bank resulting in a 10-year note payable bearing 12% interest, payable semiannually on June 1 and December 1.	Click **Make General Journal Entries** from the Company menu. Enter the date and press Tab. Tab to accept the journal entry number. Select the account from the drop-down list and press Tab or click in the Debit column. Enter the Debit amount. Click in the account column and select the next account. The credit amount displays. If this is incorrect, click in the credit column and correct the entry. Click **Save & Close**.
Dec. 1	Issue Check # 500 to The Runners Newspaper for $200 for newspaper advertising.	Click **Write Checks** icon in the Banking section of the Home Page Click the **To Print** checkbox beneath the check face. Enter the Check Number **500**, press Tab. Enter the date of the transaction, press Tab. Type **The Runners Newspaper** for Pay to the Order of and press the Tab key. Click **QuickAdd**, click **Vendor**, and click **OK**. Enter the amount. Click the drop-down list in the Account column and select the expense account. Tab to the Memo column and enter **Newspaper Advertising**. Click **Save & Close**.

Dec. 2	Sold merchandise on account to String Stores. The invoice is number 6202 and is for $4,000, terms 1/10 n/30. Runners Corporation uses a perpetual inventory system and therefore records the cost of merchandise sold as well as the sale.
	 Items sold:
	     Item # 105 – 40 pairs
	     Item # 130 – 20 pairs
		Click **Create Invoices** icon in the Customer section of the Home Page
		 Select customer from the drop-down list.
		 Select Intuit Product Invoice from the template drop-down list.
		 Enter the date of transaction
		 Enter the invoice number.
		 Click the drop-down list arrow for Terms, click **Add New**
		 Type the name **1% 10, Net 30**
		 Enter **30** as the number of days for Net Due
		 Enter **1%** as the Discount Percentage (Make sure you enter the percent sign!)
		 Enter **10** as the number of days for the discount period, click **OK**
		 Enter the Quantity.
		 Click the drop-down list in the Item column and select the first inventory item. The price each and the amount displays.
		 Enter the quantity and select the next item to complete the invoice.
		 The sales invoice displays as follows:

Date	Transaction	Instruction

Screen Shot

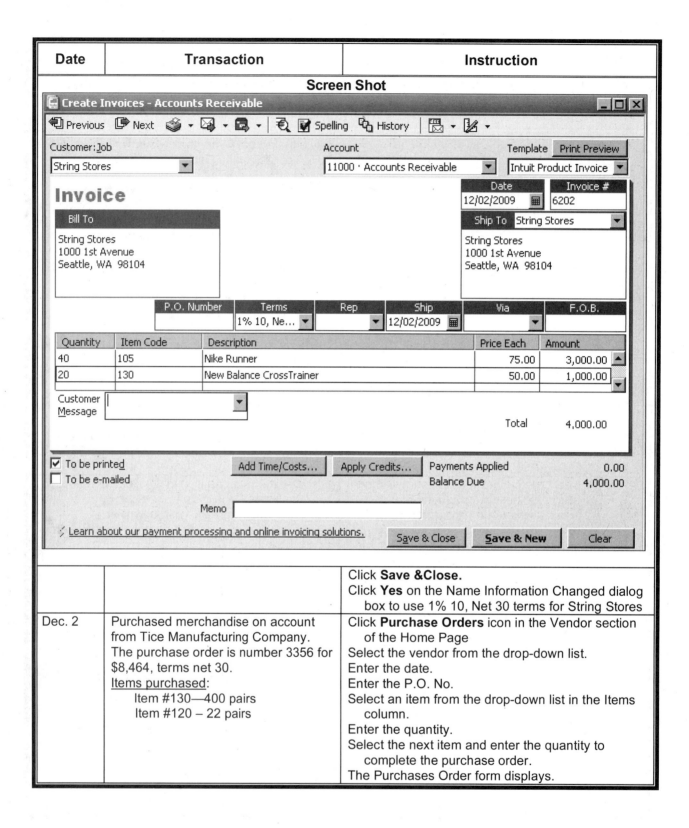

		Click **Save &Close.**
		Click **Yes** on the Name Information Changed dialog box to use 1% 10, Net 30 terms for String Stores
Dec. 2	Purchased merchandise on account from Tice Manufacturing Company. The purchase order is number 3356 for $8,464, terms net 30. <u>Items purchased:</u> Item #130—400 pairs Item #120 – 22 pairs	Click **Purchase Orders** icon in the Vendor section of the Home Page Select the vendor from the drop-down list. Enter the date. Enter the P.O. No. Select an item from the drop-down list in the Items column. Enter the quantity. Select the next item and enter the quantity to complete the purchase order. The Purchases Order form displays.

Date	Transaction	Instruction

Screen Shot

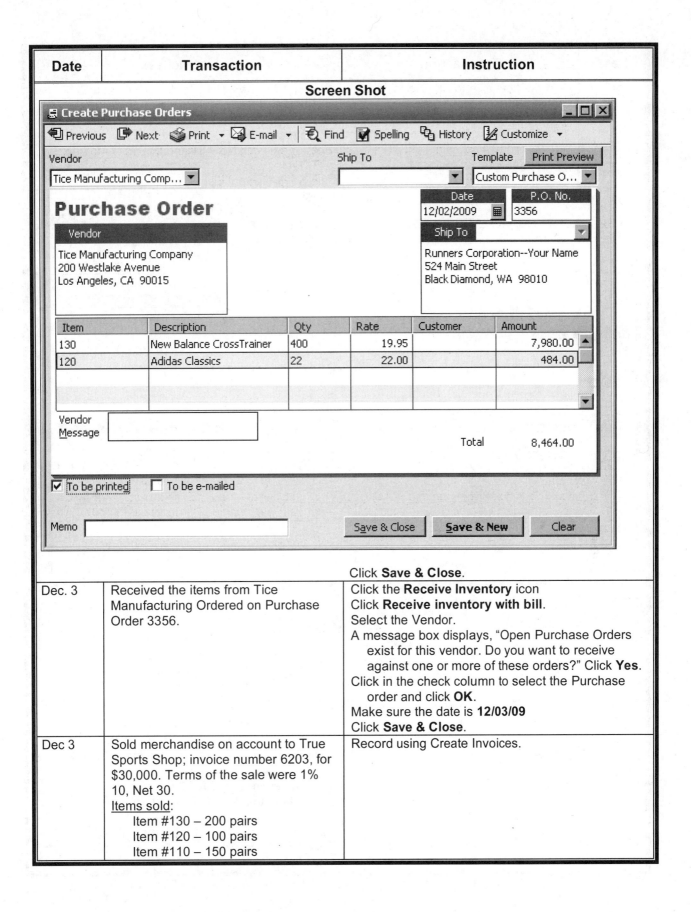

Click **Save & Close**.

Date	Transaction	Instruction
Dec. 3	Received the items from Tice Manufacturing Ordered on Purchase Order 3356.	Click the **Receive Inventory** icon Click **Receive inventory with bill**. Select the Vendor. A message box displays, "Open Purchase Orders exist for this vendor. Do you want to receive against one or more of these orders?" Click **Yes**. Click in the check column to select the Purchase order and click **OK**. Make sure the date is **12/03/09** Click **Save & Close**.
Dec 3	Sold merchandise on account to True Sports Shop; invoice number 6203, for $30,000. Terms of the sale were 1% 10, Net 30. Items sold: Item #130 – 200 pairs Item #120 – 100 pairs Item #110 – 150 pairs	Record using Create Invoices.

Date	Transaction	Instruction
Dec. 6	Sold merchandise to S.T. Sporting for cash, $18,500, check no. 481. Items sold: Item #105 – 100 pairs Item #110 – 50 pairs Item #120 – 100 pairs	Click the **Create Sales Receipts** icon in the Customer section of the Home Page Enter the name, date, and items as previously instructed Enter the Check No. **481** and Payment Method **Check** The Sales Receipt displays.

Screen Shot

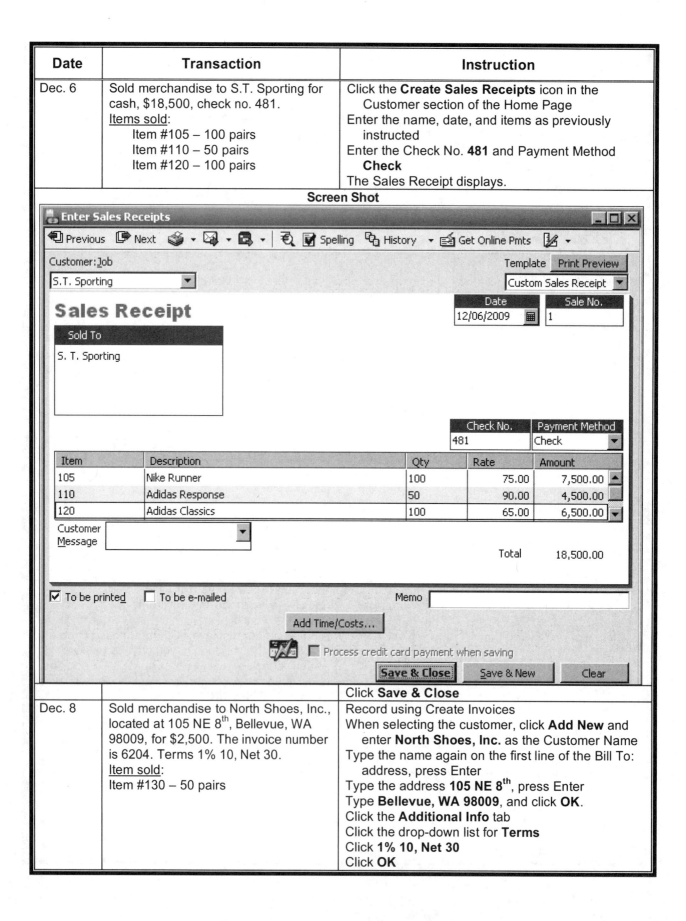

		Click **Save & Close**
Dec. 8	Sold merchandise to North Shoes, Inc., located at 105 NE 8th, Bellevue, WA 98009, for $2,500. The invoice number is 6204. Terms 1% 10, Net 30. Item sold: Item #130 – 50 pairs	Record using Create Invoices When selecting the customer, click **Add New** and enter **North Shoes, Inc.** as the Customer Name Type the name again on the first line of the Bill To: address, press Enter Type the address **105 NE 8th**, press Enter Type **Bellevue, WA 98009**, and click **OK**. Click the **Additional Info** tab Click the drop-down list for **Terms** Click **1% 10, Net 30** Click **OK**

Date	Transaction	Instruction
Dec. 8	Received a check no. 255 from All Sporting for $4,000 in payment of invoice number 6192.	Record using Receive Payments
Dec. 9	Received a check no. 898 from String Stores for $3,960. In payment of invoice number is 6202. A sales discount of $40 was taken.	Record using Receive Payments Enter the name, date, amount, payment method, and check number Click the **Discount & Credits** button. Verify the discount amount of **40**. Enter 41500 for the Sales Discount account number. Click Done to return to the payment window. View the payment information

Screen Shot

Click **Save & Close**

Date	Transaction	Instruction

Dec. 9	Purchased merchandise from Tic Manufacturing Company. The purchase order number 3357 for $23,350.
	Items purchased:
	    Item #105 – 400 pairs
	    Item #110 – 350 pairs
	    Item #120 – 50 pairs
		Record using Create Purchase Orders

Date	Transaction	Instruction
Dec. 9	Returned $1,300 worth of merchandise to Say Manufacturing Company,. Received a credit memorandum, CM1004, acknowledging a reduction in the liability account of $1,300. Item returned: Item #105 – 52 pairs	Click the **Enter Bills** icon Click **Credit**. Select the vendor. Enter the date. Enter **CM1004** for the Ref. No. Enter the amount. Click the Items tab. Select the item and enter the quantity. Click **Save & Close**.
Dec 10	Received the items from Tic Manufacturing Company, Purchase Order 3357. Terms Net 30.	Record the receipt of the items with a bill using Receive Items
Dec. 10	Received check no. 305 from True Sports Shop, for $29,700 in payment of invoice number 6203, sales discount $300.	Record using Receive Payments Be sure to click the **Discount & Credits** button. Verify the discount amount and account used. If correct, click **Done** to return to the payment window. Click **Save & Close**
Dec. 10	Sold merchandise to Hale Sporting Goods for cash (check no. 442), $9,750. Items sold: Item #105—130 pairs	Record using Create Sales Receipts Be sure to enter the check number and select the payment method of check.
Dec. 13	Pay Hoot Manufacturing $18,000 in payment of invoice number 3532. Issue Check # 501	Click the **Pay Bills** icon Click in the check box to mark the invoice for Hoot Manufacturing. Enter the date Select **Check** for payment method. Click assign check no. Click **Pay Selected Bills**. Enter the check number and click **OK**. Click **Done**
Dec. 14	Received $70,000 for the sale of 50,000 shares of $1 par value common stock.	Use Make General Journal Entries from the Company menu.
Dec. 15	Received check no. 678 from North Shoes, Inc. for $2,475, invoice number 6204. A sales discount of $25 was taken by North Shoes.	Record using Receive Payments Be sure to click the **Discount & Credits** button. Verify the discount amount and account used. If correct, click **Done** to return to the payment window. Click **Save & Close**.
Dec. 17	Issue Check # 502 to Hay Manufacturing Company for $33,000, purchase invoice number 3533.	Record using Pay Bills
Dec. 20	The city council donated land with a fair market value of $5,000 to Runners Corporation as an incentive for future expansion.	Use Make General Journal Entries from the Company menu. If you get a message regarding tracking fixed assets, click **OK**

Date	Transaction	Instruction
Dec. 21	Issue Check # 503 to Say Manufacturing Company for $935 in partial payment of purchase invoice number 3534. Apply the Credit of $1,300.	Record using Pay Bills. Click **Set Credit** and click **Done** to display the credit. Enter the partial payment amount in the Amt. to Pay column, and press Tab. Be sure to enter the date. Click **Pay Selected Bills**. Enter the check number, click **OK** and **Done**
Dec. 22	Issue Check # 504 to All Insurance Company for $3,000. The payment represents next year's insurance coverage.	Record using Write Checks. Add the new vendor and select the asset account to apply the payment. Enter the Memo: **Insurance for the Year**
Dec. 27	Runners Corporation sold land for $4,500 cash; no gain or loss	Use Make General Journal Entries from the Company menu.
Dec. 28	Issue Check # 505 to Bell Advertising Agency for $4,000.	Record using Write Checks Add the new vendor and select the expense account
Dec. 28	Sold marketable securities for $25,000. Recognize a gain of $5,000.	Use Make General Journal Entries from the Company menu.
Dec 30	Issue Check # 506 to U. S. Post Office for $100. (Charge to miscellaneous expense)	Record using Write Checks. Add the new vendor and select the expense account
Dec. 30	Issue Check # 507 to the City of Black Diamond for $350 for payment of utility bill.	Record using Write Checks Add the new vendor and select the expense account
Dec. 30	Purchased additional land for further plant expansion. Issue Check # 508 for $20,000 to Mary Realty.	Record using Write Checks Add the new vendor and select the asset account.
Dec. 30	Declared and paid a special year-end 10 cents per share on the 150,000 shares of stock outstanding. Issue Check # 509.	Use Write Checks to record the use of Check 509. Leave the Pay to the Order Of: blank Use Retained Earnings, Beginning as the account. Enter the Memo: **Paid 10 Cents Per Share Dividend on 150,000 Shares of Stock**
Dec. 30	Tog Sport Shop notified us of their bankruptcy proceeding. This makes it necessary to write off their account as uncollectible. QuickBooks uses the Direct write off method.	Use Make General Journal Entries from the Company menu Enter the date of the transaction Debit 60800 Uncollectible Accounts Expense Credit 11000 Accounts Receivable and enter Tog Sport Shop in the Name column. Click **Save & Close**.
Dec. 30	Sold merchandise on account to String Stores. The invoice is number 6205 and is for $1,000, terms 1/10 n/30. <u>items sold:</u> Item #130 – 20 pairs	Record using Create Invoices.
Dec. 30	Deposits Receipts	Click the **Record Deposits** icon in the Banking Section of the Home Page Click **Select All**. Click **OK**. Verify that **10100 Cash** is the account used and that the date is **12/30/09** Click **Save & Close**.
	BACKUP DATA files before entering adjusting entries.	See Appendix D for instructions. Name the file: **Runners Corporation (Backup Before Adj)**

End of Year Instructions

December 31st, is the last business day of the calendar year. You will need to proceed with the work required at the close of the annual accounting period as follows:

Printing Reports before Adjustments

Name of Report	Instruction	Check Figures
General Journal	Select **Accountant & Taxes** from the Reports Center. Click **Journal**. Enter the dates **12/01/09** through **12/31/09** Press Tab.	$530,147.50
General Ledger	Select **Accountant & Taxes** from the Reports Center. Click **General Ledger**. Enter the dates **12/01/09** through **12/31/09** Press Tab.	Cash Balance is $198,375.00
Trial Balance	Select **Accountant & Taxes** from the Reports Center. Click **Trial Balance**. Enter the dates **12/01/09** through **12/31/09** Press Tab.	$870,774.00

Entering Adjusting Entries

Enter the following adjusting entries using the General Journal Entry from the Tasks menu.

1. The physical inventory of merchandise at the close of business, December 31, 2009, showed $25,822.50, consisting of:
   Item #105 Quantity on Hand 250 pairs
   Item #110 Quantity on Hand 320 pairs
   Item #120 Quantity on Hand 172 pairs
   Item #130 Quantity on Hand 230 pairs
   a. To enter the adjustment to the Inventory Account click the **Adjust Quantity on Hand** icon in the company section of the Home Page
   b. Click the **Value Adjustment** text box
   c. Create and select a new expense account for the adjustment: **61100 Inventory Adjustment Expense**
   d. Enter the quantities shown above for each of the inventory items and press Tab
   d. Note the total value adjustment of **-1,351**
   e. Click **Save & Close**

Note: For the following adjusting entries use Make General Journal Entries from the Company menu. Refer to the Trial Balance to verify adjustment accounts.

2. Office supplies on hand on December 31, $1,500.
3. Insurance expired for the month of December, $250.
4. Depreciation expense for the year 2009: (You can enter a compound entry)
   a. Office equipment $8,535
   b. Building $7,500
5. Accrued salaries at December 31, $7,000; do not record payroll tax accruals.
6. Accrued interest at December 31, $400.

7. Accrued property tax for the months of November and December, payable in April, 2009, $1,139.
8. Amortization of organization costs, $1,000.
9. The income tax for 2009 is $24,000.

Reports for Year End

Use the Report Center to Prepare the Year End Reports. Compare your totals with the check figures and print if instructed to do so by your professor.

Name of Report	Instructions	Check Figures
General Journal	Select **Accountant & Taxes** Click **Journal**. Enter the dates **12/01/09** to **12/31/09** Press Tab.	$582,221.50
General Ledger	Select **Accountant & Taxes** Click **General Ledger**. Enter the dates **12/01/09** to **12/31/09** Press Tab.	Cash balance is $198,375.00
Trial Balance	Select **Accountant & Taxes** Click **Trial Balance**. Enter the dates **12/01/09** to **12/31/09** Press Tab.	$919,348.00
Income Statement	Select **Company & Financial** Click **Profit and Loss Standard**. Enter the dates **01/01/09** to **12/31/09** to prepare the report for the year Press Tab.	$96,989.50
Balance Sheet	Select **Company & Financial** Click **Balance Sheet Standard**. Enter the date **12/31/09** Press Tab.	$433,452.50
Cash Flow Statement	Select **Company and Financials** Click **Statement of Cash Flows**. Enter the dates **01/01/09** to **12/31/09** to prepare the report for the year Press Tab.	Operating Activities, $164,818.00 Investing Activities, $-195,105.00 Financing Activities, $228,662.00
Aged Receivables	Click **Customers & Receivables** Click **A/R Aging Detail**. Enter the date **12/31/09** Press Tab.	$9,650
Aged Payables	Click **Vendors & Payables** Click **A/P Aging Detail**. Enter the date **12/31/09** Press Tab.	$35,382.00

If all balances are correct, then refer to **Appendix D** to backup your data files. If not review the General Journal and correct any transactions using instructions in **Appendix C**.

CHAPTER 5

In this chapter, you will begin installing the Peachtree Complete 2008 or 2009 Data Files for Runners Corporation. Then you will record the transactions for December using the Company, Customer & Sales, Vendor & Purchases, and Banking Tasks. To become familiar with the Peachtree Complete 2008 or 2009 environment, refer to Appendix B.

Installation of Runners Corporation – Peachtree Complete 2008 or 2009 Data File

The Runners Corporation data file used in completing the practice set is on the CD-ROM that accompanies this text.

Installation Procedure: Peachtree Complete 2008 or 2009

To place the Runners' Corporation practice set data files for use with Peachtree onto your computer's hard disk, follow these instructions:

1. Start Windows.
2. Make sure that no other programs are running on your system.
3. Insert the CD-ROM into your CD-ROM drive.
4. Click on the Start button; then click on Run.
5. Type d:\start.exe and press the ENTER key, where "d" stands for the letter of your computer's CD-ROM drive.
6. From the CD's opening screen, click on the Install button.
7. From the Install screen, click on Peachtree Complete Accounting 2008 or 2009 Practice Sets. Files will extract to C:\Peachtree2009 on your computer; you may change this default directory designation if desired, when prompted.
8. Put your CD-ROM away for safekeeping
9. Exit the CD.

Student Data File Integrity

Peachtree Complete Accounting 2008 or 2009 will run most efficiently if the Runners Corporation data file is installed on a hard drive. This can occur on the local hard drive or in a unique student folder on a network drive. It is recommended that students back up files each class day and at selected points in the training. Peachtree Complete Accounting's back up and restore functions are quick and easy. The specific procedures will be discussed within the instructions and in Appendix B.

Using Peachtree Complete Accounting 2008 or 2009 on a Network

Peachtree Accounting can be used in a network environment as long as each student uses a separate Student Data File source to store his or her data file. Students should consult with their instructor and/or network administrator for specific procedures regarding program installation and any special printing procedures required for proper network operation.

Opening Runners Corporation –
Peachtree Complete 2008 or 2009 Data Files

1. Click on the Start button. Point to **Programs**; point to the **Peachtree Complete Accounting** folder and select **Peachtree Complete Accounting**. Your desktop may have the Peachtree icon allowing for a quicker entrance into the program by double-clicking it.
2. From the Peachtree Accounting dialog box, click "**Open an existing Company**." The Open an existing company dialog box displays:

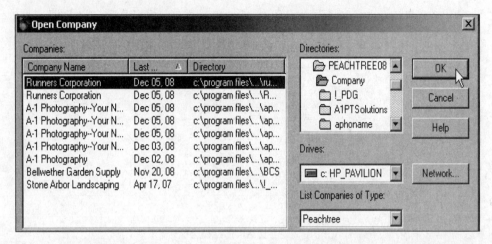

3. Select **Runners Corporation** and click **OK**. If Runners Corporation does not appear, click the Browse button and locate the folder C:\Peachtree2009. If a message displays requesting running a "Year-End Wizard", click No. Runners Corporation appears in the title bar of the main window.

Displaying Trial Balance, General Ledger, Accounts Receivable, and Accounts Payable Balances

It is important for you to be able to identify the specific reports that you print for each assignment as your own, particularly if you are using a computer that shares a printer with other computers. Peachtree Complete Accounting 2008 or 2009 prints the name of the company you are working with at the top of each report. To personalize your reports so that you can identify both the company and your printed reports, the company name needs to be modified.

1. Click on **Maintain** menu option. Then select **Company Information**. The program will respond by bringing up a dialog box allowing the user to edit/add information about the company.
2. Click in the **Company Name** entry field at the end of **Runners Corporation**. If it is already highlighted, press the right arrow key.
3. Add a dash and your name "**-Student Name**" or initials to the end of the company name. Your screen will look similar to the one shown below:

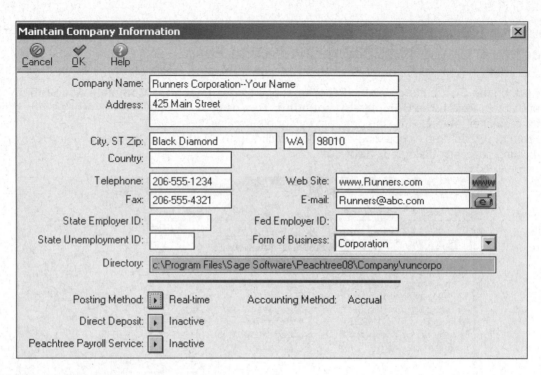

Click **OK** to close window.
4. Click **Reports & Forms** menu option. Select **General Ledger**.
   a. Double-click **Chart of Accounts** to view the account list. Click the close button.
   b. Double-click **General Ledger** and verify the balances. Click the close button.
   c. Double-click **General Ledger Trial Balance**. The Trial balance displays:

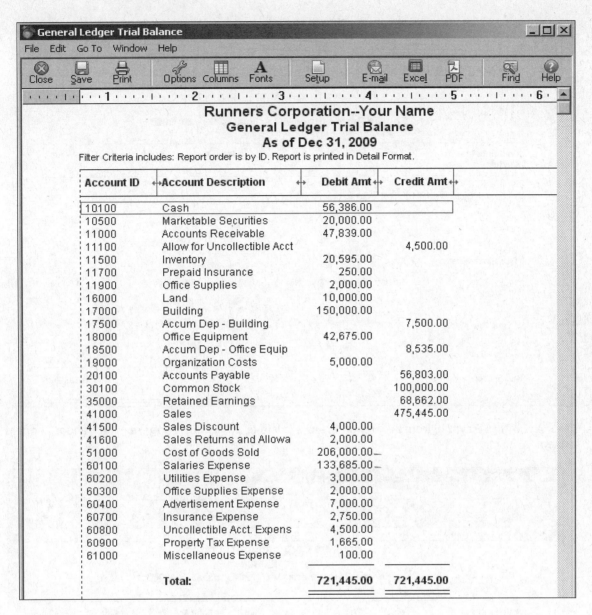

File   Edit   Go To   Window   Help

Close   Save   Print   Options   Columns   Fonts   Setup   E-mail   Excel   PDF   Find   Help

Runners Corporation--Your Name
General Ledger Trial Balance
As of Dec 31, 2009

Filter Criteria includes: Report order is by ID. Report is printed in Detail Format.

Account ID	Account Description	Debit Amt	Credit Amt
10100	Cash	56,386.00	
10500	Marketable Securities	20,000.00	
11000	Accounts Receivable	47,839.00	
11100	Allow for Uncollectible Acct		4,500.00
11500	Inventory	20,595.00	
11700	Prepaid Insurance	250.00	
11900	Office Supplies	2,000.00	
16000	Land	10,000.00	
17000	Building	150,000.00	
17500	Accum Dep - Building		7,500.00
18000	Office Equipment	42,675.00	
18500	Accum Dep - Office Equip		8,535.00
19000	Organization Costs	5,000.00	
20100	Accounts Payable		56,803.00
30100	Common Stock		100,000.00
35000	Retained Earnings		68,662.00
41000	Sales		475,445.00
41500	Sales Discount	4,000.00	
41600	Sales Returns and Allowa	2,000.00	
51000	Cost of Goods Sold	206,000.00	
60100	Salaries Expense	133,685.00	
60200	Utilities Expense	3,000.00	
60300	Office Supplies Expense	2,000.00	
60400	Advertisement Expense	7,000.00	
60700	Insurance Expense	2,750.00	
60800	Uncollectible Acct. Expens	4,500.00	
60900	Property Tax Expense	1,665.00	
61000	Miscellaneous Expense	100.00	
	Total:	**721,445.00**	**721,445.00**

Click the close button after viewing.

5. Click **Accounts Receivable** from the Report area. Double-click **Customer Ledgers**. The Customer Ledgers appear:

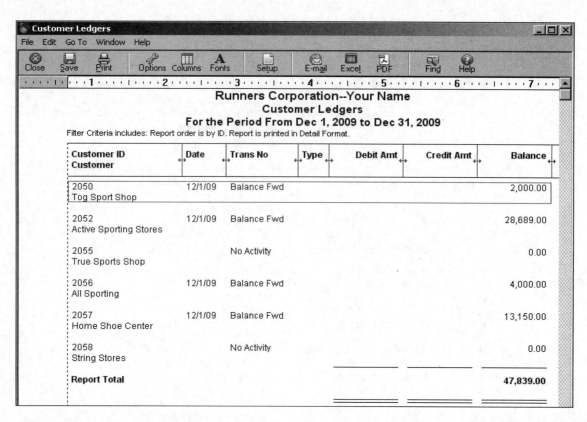

6. Click **Accounts Payable** from the Report area. Double click **Vendor Ledgers**. The Vendor Ledgers appear:

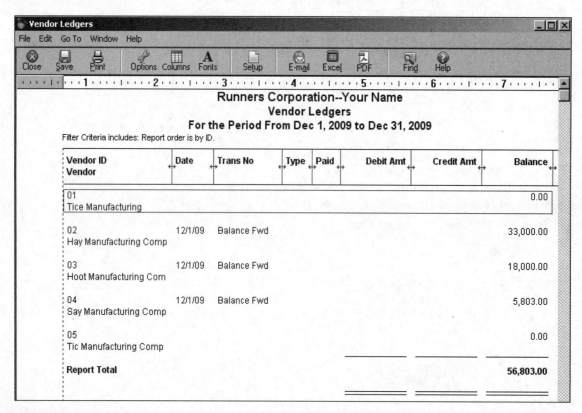

After viewing close the window.

Any of the reports can be printed by clicking the **Print** button from the menu bar of the displayed report. Note that each report's heading includes your name.

Computerizing Runners Corporation Using Peachtree

The business transactions for Runners Corporation are displayed on the following pages. Peachtree Complete 2008 or 2009 should be open with Runners Corporation displaying on the title barThe Peachtree Desktop displays containing the Business Status Center.

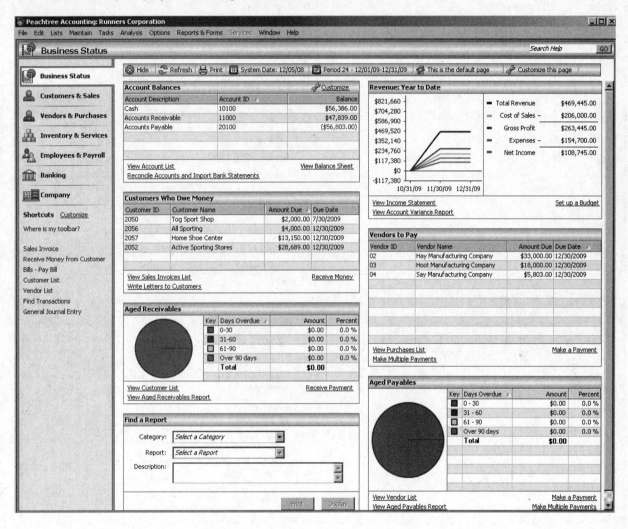

Entering Transactions

Below are the December 2009 transactions for Runners Corporation. The date, transaction description and instruction are listed. The instruction column will direct you to record each transaction in the appropriate journal. Occasionally, there will be screen shots placed within the transactions to show you how your screen should look.

Date	Transaction	Instruction
Dec. 1	Received check no. 202 from Active Sporting Stores, customer number 2052, for $28,689 in full settlement of the account.	To record a customer receipt, Peachtree offers two options: 1. Click **Receipts** from the Tasks Menu or; 2. Click **Customer & Sales** from Navigation Bar on the left. Click the **Receive Money Icon** then select **Receive money from Customer.** The Receipts window displays. Click **OK** to accept the Cash account. • Enter **12/01/09** in Deposit Ticket field. • Click the Magnifying glass button and select Active Sporting Stores. All outstanding invoices will display. • Enter check no. 202 in the reference field. • Enter the date of the transaction. • Click in the box in the Pay column. • The receipt amount displays.

Screen Shot

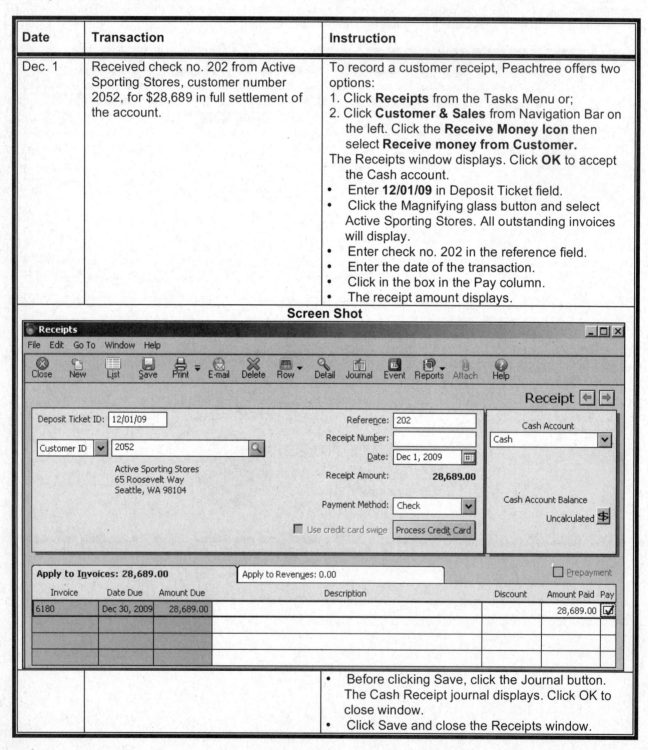

		• Before clicking Save, click the Journal button. The Cash Receipt journal displays. Click OK to close window. • Click Save and close the Receipts window.

Date	Transaction	Instruction
Dec. 1	Borrowed $40,000 from State Bank resulting in a 10-year note payable bearing 12% interest, payable semiannually on June 1 and December 1.	To record the transaction in the **General Journal**, Peachtree offers two options: 1. Click **General Journal Entry** from the Task Menu; or 2. Click **Banking** from the Navigation Bar on the left. Click **General Journal Entry Icon** then click **New General Journal Entry**. • Enter the date of the transaction. • Enter "State Bank" in the reference field. • Click the Magnifying Glass button and select the general ledger account. • Enter "10 year note payable, 12% June 1 & Dec. 1" in the description field. • Enter the amount in the Debit column. • Select the account to credit, the description will display, then enter the amount in the credit column. • Click Save and close the window.
Dec. 1	Issue Check # 500 to The Runners Newspaper for $200 for newspaper advertising.	To write a check, Peachtree offers two options: 1. Click **Write Checks** from the Tasks Menu or; 2. Click **Banking** from the Navigation Bar on the left. Click the **Write Check Icon** then click **New Check**. The Write Check window displays. The account is **Cash**. • Click the Magnifying Glass button. • Click the **New** button to add the new vendor. • Enter **06** for Vendor number • Enter **Runners Newspaper** for the Vendor Name. • On the **General** tab, select **60400 Advertisement Expense** for the Expense Account using the Magnifying Glass button. • Click **Save** and close the window. • Select the **Vendor**. • Enter the **Check Number**. • Enter the **Date**. • Enter the **Amount**. • Enter "**Newspaper Advertising**" for the memo. • Click **Save** and close.

Dec. 2	Sold merchandise on account to String Stores, customer number 2058. The sales invoice is number 6202 and is for $4,000, terms 1/10 n/30. Runners Corporation uses a perpetual inventory system and therefore records the cost of merchandise sold as well as the sale.
	Items sold:
	    Item # 105 – 40 pairs
	    Item # 130 – 20 pairs
		To record a sales invoice, Peachtree offers two options: 1. Click **Sales/Invoicing** from the Tasks menu or; 2. Click **Customer & Sales** from the Navigation Bar on the left. Click **Sales Invoice Icon** then **New Sales Invoice**. The Sales Order window will display.
		• Click the Magnifying Glass button to select the **Customer**.
		• Enter the **Date** of transaction.
		• Enter the invoice number in **Invoice No.** box.
		• Enter the **Quantity** and press tab.
		• Click the Magnifying Glass button and select the

Date	Transaction	Instruction
		Item Number. • Press tab and the unit price and extended amount will display. • Enter the next item. • The sales invoice displays below:

Screen shot

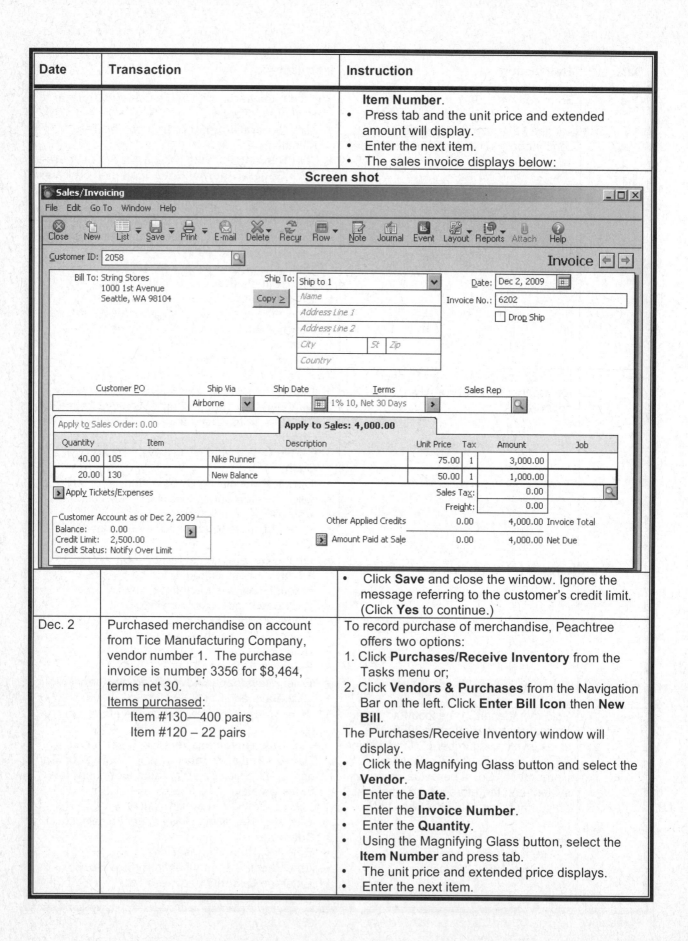

		• Click **Save** and close the window. Ignore the message referring to the customer's credit limit. (Click **Yes** to continue.)
Dec. 2	Purchased merchandise on account from Tice Manufacturing Company, vendor number 1. The purchase invoice is number 3356 for $8,464, terms net 30. Items purchased: Item #130—400 pairs Item #120 – 22 pairs	To record purchase of merchandise, Peachtree offers two options: 1. Click **Purchases/Receive Inventory** from the Tasks menu or; 2. Click **Vendors & Purchases** from the Navigation Bar on the left. Click **Enter Bill Icon** then **New Bill**. The Purchases/Receive Inventory window will display. • Click the Magnifying Glass button and select the **Vendor**. • Enter the **Date**. • Enter the **Invoice Number**. • Enter the **Quantity**. • Using the Magnifying Glass button, select the **Item Number** and press tab. • The unit price and extended price displays. • Enter the next item.

Date	Transaction	Instruction
		• The Purchases/Receive Inventory form displays.

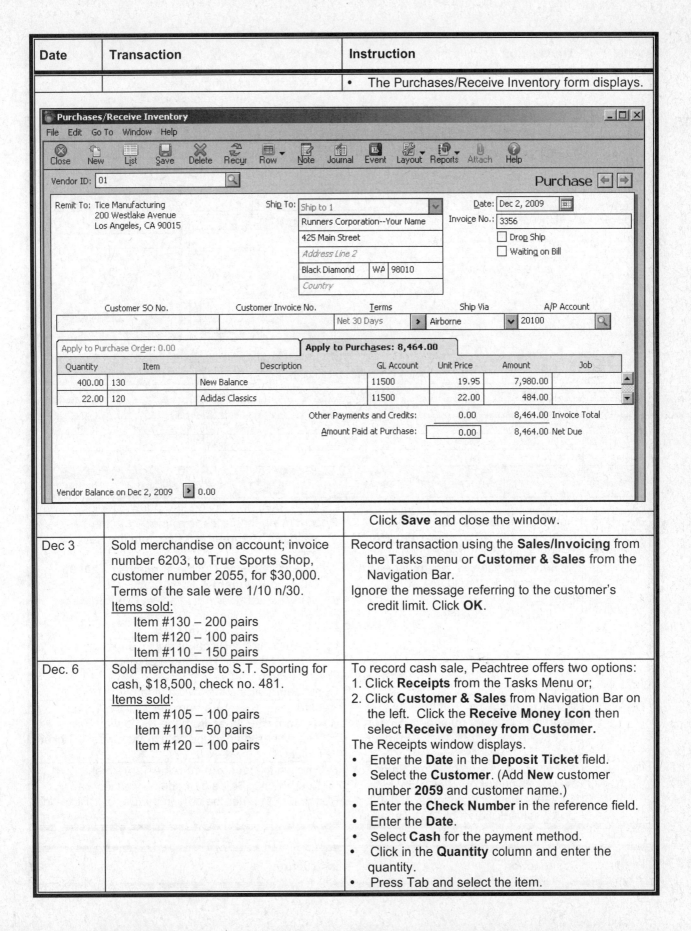

		Click **Save** and close the window.
Dec 3	Sold merchandise on account; invoice number 6203, to True Sports Shop, customer number 2055, for $30,000. Terms of the sale were 1/10 n/30. Items sold: Item #130 – 200 pairs Item #120 – 100 pairs Item #110 – 150 pairs	Record transaction using the **Sales/Invoicing** from the Tasks menu or **Customer & Sales** from the Navigation Bar. Ignore the message referring to the customer's credit limit. Click **OK**.
Dec. 6	Sold merchandise to S.T. Sporting for cash, $18,500, check no. 481. Items sold: Item #105 – 100 pairs Item #110 – 50 pairs Item #120 – 100 pairs	To record cash sale, Peachtree offers two options: 1. Click **Receipts** from the Tasks Menu or; 2. Click **Customer & Sales** from Navigation Bar on the left. Click the **Receive Money Icon** then select **Receive money from Customer.** The Receipts window displays. • Enter the **Date** in the **Deposit Ticket** field. • Select the **Customer**. (Add **New** customer number **2059** and customer name.) • Enter the **Check Number** in the reference field. • Enter the **Date**. • Select **Cash** for the payment method. • Click in the **Quantity** column and enter the quantity. • Press Tab and select the item.

Date	Transaction	Instruction
		• Enter the remaining items. • The completed receipts form displays.

Screen Shot

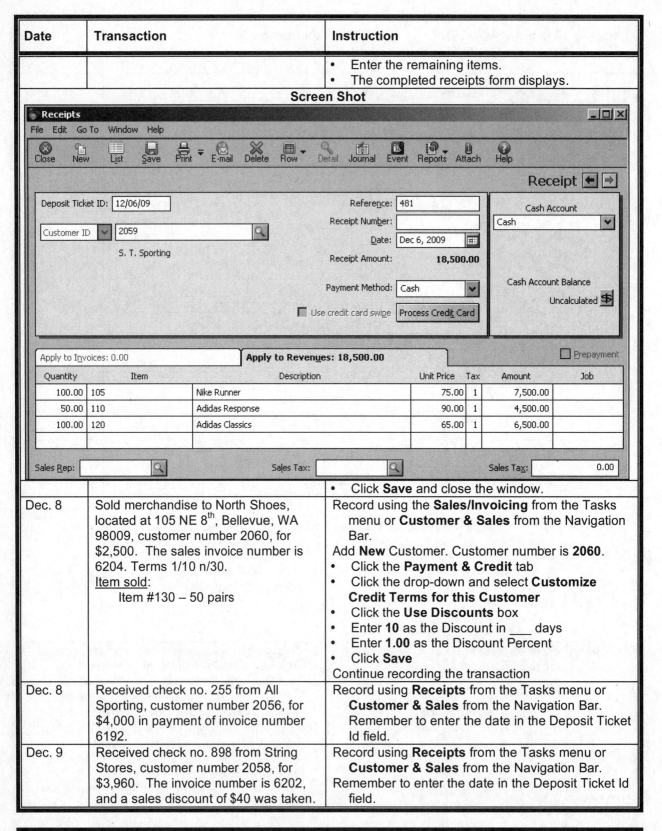

Date	Transaction	Instruction
		• Click **Save** and close the window.
Dec. 8	Sold merchandise to North Shoes, located at 105 NE 8th, Bellevue, WA 98009, customer number 2060, for $2,500. The sales invoice number is 6204. Terms 1/10 n/30. <u>Item sold:</u> Item #130 – 50 pairs	Record using the **Sales/Invoicing** from the Tasks menu or **Customer & Sales** from the Navigation Bar. Add **New** Customer. Customer number is **2060**. • Click the **Payment & Credit** tab • Click the drop-down and select **Customize Credit Terms for this Customer** • Click the **Use Discounts** box • Enter **10** as the Discount in ___ days • Enter **1.00** as the Discount Percent • Click **Save** Continue recording the transaction
Dec. 8	Received check no. 255 from All Sporting, customer number 2056, for $4,000 in payment of invoice number 6192.	Record using **Receipts** from the Tasks menu or **Customer & Sales** from the Navigation Bar. Remember to enter the date in the Deposit Ticket Id field.
Dec. 9	Received check no. 898 from String Stores, customer number 2058, for $3,960. The invoice number is 6202, and a sales discount of $40 was taken.	Record using **Receipts** from the Tasks menu or **Customer & Sales** from the Navigation Bar. Remember to enter the date in the Deposit Ticket Id field.

Date	Transaction	Instruction

Date	Transaction	Instruction
Dec. 9	Purchased merchandise from Tic Manufacturing Company, vendor number 5. The purchase invoice is number 3538 for $23,350. Terms 30 days. Items purchased: Item #105 – 400 pairs Item #110 – 350 pairs Item #120 – 50 pairs	Record using **Purchase/Receive** Inventory from the Tasks menu or **Vendor & Purchases** from the Navigation Bar.
Dec. 9	Returned $1,300 worth of merchandise to Say Manufacturing Company, vendor 4. Received a credit memorandum acknowledging a reduction in the liability account of $1,300. Item returned: Item #105 – 52 pairs	To record vendor credit, Peachtree offers two options: 1. Click **Vendor Credit Memos** from the Tasks menu or; 2. Click **Vendors & Purchases** from the Navigation Bar on the left. Click **Credits and Returns Icon** then **New Vendor Credit Memo.** The Vendors Credit Memo window will display. • Select the **Vendor**. • Enter the **Date**. • Enter **CM1004** for the Credit No. • Click the **Apply to Purchases** Tab. • Enter the **Quantity**. • Select the **Item** and press tab. • The credit amount will display. • **Save** and close the window.
Dec 10	Received check no. 305 from True Sports Shop, customer number 2055, for $29,700 in payment of invoice number 6203, sales discount $300.	Record using **Receipts** from the Tasks menu or **Customer & Sales** from the Navigation Bar.
Dec. 10	Cash sale of merchandise to Hale Sporting Goods (check no. 442), $9,750. Items sold: Item #105—130 pairs	Record using **Sales/Invoicing** from the Tasks menu or **Customer & Sales** from the Navigation Bar. Add customer number 2061 and customer name.
Dec. 13	Issue Check No. 501 to Hoot Manufacturing, Vendor Number 3, for $18,000 in payment of Purchase Invoice Number 3532.	Record using **Payments** from the Tasks menu or **Pay Bills** in the **Vendors & Purchases** section of the Navigation Bar.
Dec. 14	Received $70,000 for the sale of 50,000 shares of $1 par value common stock.	To record the transaction in the **General Journal**, Peachtree offers two options: 1. Click **General Journal Entry** from the Task Menu; or 2. Click **General Journal Entry Icon** from the Navigation Bar then click **New General Journal Entry**. In the reference field, enter **Sale of CS**. Enter "**Sale of Common Stock**" in Description column.
Dec. 15	Received check no. 678 from North Shoes, customer number 2060, for $2,475, invoice number 6204. A sales discount of $25 was taken.	Record using **Receipts** from the Tasks menu or **Customer & Sales** from the Navigation Bar.
Dec. 17	Issue Check # 502 to Hay	Record using **Payments** from the Tasks menu or

Date	Transaction	Instruction
	Manufacturing Company, vendor number 2, for $33,000, purchase invoice number 3533.	**Vendors & Purchases** from the Navigation Bar.
Dec. 20	The city council donated land with a fair market value of $5,000 to Runners Corporation as an incentive for future expansion.	To record the transaction in the **General Journal**, Peachtree offers two options: 1. Click **General Journal Entry** from the Task Menu; or 2. Click **General Journal Entry Icon** from the Navigation Bar then click **New General Journal Entry**. Enter "**Donated Land**" in Reference field. Enter "**City Council Donation of Land**" in the description column.
Dec. 21	Issue Check # 503 to Say Manufacturing Company, vendor number 4, for $935 in partial payment of purchase invoice number 3534.	Record using **Payments** from the Tasks menu or **Vendors & Purchases** from the Navigation Bar. Enter the **Amount Paid** of **935.00**, press **Tab** and the check box will be checked.
Dec. 22	Issue Check # 504 to All Insurance Company for $3,000. The payment represents next year's insurance coverage.	Record using **Write Checks** from the Tasks menu or **Banking** from the Navigation Bar. Add a **New** vendor using number **07**. Enter the **Prepaid Insurance** as the expense account for the vendor. Enter "**Purchase of Insurance**" in the memo field.
Dec. 27	Runners Corporation sold land for $4,500 cash; no gain or loss was recognized.	To record the transaction in the **General Journal**, Peachtree offers two options: 1. Click **General Journal Entry** from the Task Menu; or 2. Click **General Journal Entry Icon** then click **New General Journal Entry**. Enter "**Sold Land**" in the Reference Field. Enter "**Sold Land--No Gain or Loss**" in the description column.
Dec. 28	Issue Check # 505 to Bell Advertising Agency for $4,000.	Record using **Write Checks** from the Tasks menu or **Banking** from the Navigation Bar. Add a **New** vendor using number **08**. Enter **Advertisement Expense** as the expense account. Enter "**Advertising Expense**" in the Memo field.
Dec. 28	Sold marketable securities for $25,000. Recognize a gain of $5,000.	To record the transaction in the **General Journal**, Peachtree offers two options: 1. Click **General Journal Entry** from the Task Menu; or 2. Click **General Journal Entry Icon** from the Navigation Bar then click **New General Journal Entry**. Enter **Sold MS** in the reference field. Enter "**Sold Marketable Securities**" in the Description column.

Date	Transaction	Instruction
Dec 30	Issue Check # 506 to US Post Office for $100. (Charge to miscellaneous expense)	Record using **Write Checks** from the Tasks menu or **Banking** from the Navigation Bar. Add a **New** vendor using number **09**. Enter **Miscellaneous Expense** as the expense account. Enter **Postage** in the memo field.
Dec. 30	Issue Check # 507 to the City of Black Diamond for $350 for payment of utility bill.	Record using **Write Checks** from the Tasks menu or **Banking** from the Navigation Bar. Add a **New** vendor using number **10**. Enter **Utilities Expense** as the expense account. Enter **Utilities Expense** in the memo field
Dec. 30	Purchased additional land for further plant expansion. Issue Check # 508 for $20,000 to Mary Realty.	Record using **Write Checks** from the Tasks menu or **Banking** from the Navigation Bar. Add a **New** vendor using number **11**. Enter **Land** as the expense account. Enter **Purchased Land** in the memo field.
Dec. 30	Declared and paid a special year-end 10 cents per share on the 150,000 shares of stock outstanding. Issue Check # 509.	To record the declaration of dividends in the **General Journal,** Peachtree offers two options: 1. Click **General Journal Entry** from the Task Menu; or 2. Click **General Journal Entry Icon** from the Navigation Bar then click **New General Journal Entry**. Enter the **Ck 509 Paid Dividend** in the Reference field. Enter "**Declared and Paid Dividends at 10 Cents Per Share**" in Description column.
Dec. 30	Tog Sport Shop notified us of their bankruptcy proceeding. This makes it necessary to write off their account as uncollectible.	Record using **Receipts** from the Tasks menu or **Customer & Sales** from the Navigation Bar. Enter "**Write Off**" in the Reference field. Click the **Pay box** for the amount. In the **General Journal**, record the adjustment to the **Cash** and **Allowance for Uncollectable Accounts** to complete the write off. Use **Write Off Bad Debt—Tog Sport Shop** as the Description.
Dec. 30	Sold merchandise on account to String Stores. The sales invoice is number 6205 and is for $1,000., terms 1/10 n/30. <u>Item sold:</u> Item #130 – 20 pairs	Record using **Sales/Invoicing** from the Tasks menu or **Customer & Sales** from the Navigation Bar.
	BACKUP DATA files before entering adjusting entries.	See Appendix D for instructions

End of Year Instructions

December 31st is the last business day of the calendar year. You will need to proceed with the work required at the close of the annual accounting period as follows:

Printing Reports before Adjustments

Prior to recording the adjustments, to print the following reports, click the **Print** button at the top of the report, verify the printer, and then click **OK**.

Name of Report	Instruction	Check Figures
General Journal	Click **General Ledger** from the **Reports & Forms** menu. Double-click **General Journal** Click **OK**.	$161,500.00
General Ledger	Click General Ledger from the Reports menu. Double Click General Ledger.	Cash Balance is $198,375.00
General Ledger Trial Balance	Click General Ledger from the Reports menu. Double Click General Ledger Trial Balance.	$868,774.00

Entering Adjusting Entries

Enter the following adjusting entries using the General Journal Entry from the Tasks menu:

1. The physical inventory of merchandise at the close of business, December 31, 2009, showed $25,822.50, consisting of:

    Item #105 Quantity on Hand 250 pairs
    Item #110 Quantity on Hand 320 pairs
    Item #120 Quantity on Hand 172 pairs
    Item #130 Quantity on Hand 230 pairs

To enter the adjustment to the Inventory Account, use **Inventory Adjustments** from the Task Menu.
*   To begin, **Print** the **Inventory Valuation Report** from the Reports menu.
*   Click **Inventory Adjustments** from the Task Menu.
*   Reference is **Adjust**
*   Click the magnifying glass to select the inventory item.
*   Enter the adjusted unit amount in **Adjust Quantity By** field. Be sure to enter a *minus* if you are reducing the Quantity on Hand.
*   Enter **"Year End Physical Count"** as the reason.
*   Save and enter the next adjustment.
*   After entering all adjustments, click **Save** and close.

Note: For the following adjusting entries use **General Journal Entry** from the Tasks menu. Use **Adjusting Entry** in the Reference and the Description fields. Refer to the General Ledger Trial Balance to verify adjustment accounts.

2. Office supplies on hand on December 31, $1,500.   2,000
3. Insurance expired for the month of December, $250.
4. Depreciation expense for the year 2009: (You can enter a compound entry)
    Office equipment $8,535
    Building $7,500
5. Management has decided to increase the **Allowance for Uncollectible Accts** account by $200.
6. Accrued salaries at December 31, $7,000.
7. Accrued interest at December 31, $400.
8. Accrued property tax for the months of November and December, payable in April, 2009, $1,139.
9. Amortization of organization costs, $1,000.
10. The income tax for 2009 is $24,000.

Printing Reports for Year End

Name of Report	Instructions	Check Figures
General Journal	Click **General Ledger** from the **Reports & Forms** menu. Double-click **General Journal**.	$212,024.00 This may vary if additional entries have been entered.
General Ledger	Click **General Ledger** from the **Reports & Forms** menu. Double-click **General Ledger**.	Cash balance is $198,375.00
General Ledger Trial Balance	Click **General Ledger** from the **Reports & Forms** menu. Double-click **General Ledger Trial Balance**	$917,548.00
Income Statement	Click **Financial Statements** from the **Reports & Forms** menu. Double-click **Income Stmnt**. Click **OK** for current period.	$97,871.50 for the Year to Date
Retained Earnings	Click **Financial Statements** from the **Reports & Forms** menu. Double-click **Retained Earnings**. Click **OK** for current period.	$151,533.50
Balance Sheet	Click **Financial Statements** from the **Reports & Forms** menu. Double-click **Balance Sheet**. Click **OK** for current period.	$434,454.50
Cash Flow Statement	Click **Financial Statements** from the **Reports & Forms** menu. Double-click **Cash Flow**. Click **OK** for current period.	Year-to-Date Operating Activities, $154,199.00 Investing Activities, $-25,000.00 Financing Activities, $115,000.00
Aged Receivables	Click **Accounts Receivables** from the **Reports & Forms** menu. Double-click **Aged Receivables**.	$14,150.00
Aged Payables	Click **Accounts Payables** from the **Reports & Forms** menu. Double-click **Aged Payables**.	$35,382.00

If all balances are correct, then refer to **Appendix D** to backup your data files. If not, review the General Journal and correct any transactions using instructions in **Appendix C.**

Runners Corporation Appendix

Name_____

Section_____

Appendix A Forms

General Journal

Date	Accounts and Explanations	Posting Reference	Debit	Credit
20XX				

General Journal

Date	Accounts and Explanations	Posting Reference	Debit	Credit

General Journal

Date	Accounts and Explanations	Posting Reference	Debit	Credit

General Journal

Date	Accounts and Explanations	Posting Reference	Debit	Credit

General Journal

Date	Accounts and Explanations	Posting Reference	Debit	Credit

RUNNERS CORPORATION
CASH DISBURSEMENTS JOURNAL

Page _____

Date	Ck. No.	Account Debited	Post Ref	Sundry Accounts Dr.	Accounts Payable Dr.	Purchases Discount Cr.	Cash Cr.
20XX							

RUNNERS CORPORATION
CASH RECEIPTS JOURNAL

Page ___

Date	Cash Dr.	Sales Discount Dr.	Accounts Receivable Cr.	Sales Cr.	Sundry		
					Account Name	Post. Ref.	Amount Cr.
20XX							

RUNNERS CORPORATION
PURCHASES JOURNAL

Date	Account Credited	Date of Invoice	Invoice Number	Terms	P R	Accounts Payable Credit	Purchases Debit	Sundry—Dr.		
								Account	P R	Amount
20XX										

RUNNERS CORPORATION
SALES JOURNAL

Date		Account Debited	Terms	Invoice Number	Post Ref	Dr. Acct. Rec/ Cr. Sales
20XX						

GENERAL LEDGER

Cash

Date	Item	Post Ref	Debit	Credit	Balance	
					Debit	Credit
20XX Dec. 1	Balance	√			56,386.00	

Marketable Securities
Account Number 10500

Date	Item	Post Ref	Debit	Credit	Balance	
					Debit	Credit
20XX Dec. 1	Balance	√			20,000.00	

Accounts Receivable   **Account Number 11000**

Date	Item	Post Ref	Debit	Credit	Balance	
					Debit	Credit
20XX Dec. 1	Balance	√			47,839.00	

Allowance for Uncollectible Accounts   **Account Number 11100**

Date	Item	Post Ref	Debit	Credit	Balance	
					Debit	Credit
20XX Dec. 1	Balance	√				4,500.00

Inventory   **Account Number 11500**

Date	Item	Post Ref	Debit	Credit	Balance	
					Debit	Credit
20XX Dec. 1	Balance	√			20,595.00	

Prepaid Insurance   Account Number 11700

Date	Item	Post Ref	Debit	Credit	Balance Debit	Balance Credit
20XX Dec. 1	Balance	√			250.00	

Office Supplies   Account Number 11900

Date	Item	Post Ref	Debit	Credit	Balance Debit	Balance Credit
20XX Dec. 1	Balance	√			2,000.00	

Land   Account Number 16000

Date	Item	Post Ref	Debit	Credit	Balance Debit	Balance Credit
20XX Dec. 1	Balance	√			10,000.00	

Building   Account Number 17000

Date	Item	Post Ref	Debit	Credit	Balance Debit	Balance Credit
20XX Dec. 1	Balance	√			150,000.00	

Accumulated Depreciation—Building   Account Number 17500

Date	Item	Post Ref	Debit	Credit	Balance Debit	Balance Credit
20XX Dec. 1	Balance	√				7,500.00

Office Equipment   Account Number 18000

Date	Item	Post Ref	Debit	Credit	Balance Debit	Balance Credit
20XX Dec. 1	Balance	√			42,675.00	

Accumulated Depreciation—Office Equipment   Account Number 18500

Date	Item	Post Ref	Debit	Credit	Balance Debit	Balance Credit
20XX Dec. 1	Balance	√				8,535.00

Organization Costs   Account Number 19000

Date	Item	Post Ref	Debit	Credit	Balance Debit	Balance Credit
20XX Dec. 1	Balance	√			5,000.00	

Accounts Payable   Account Number 20100

Date	Item	Post Ref	Debit	Credit	Balance Debit	Balance Credit
20XX Dec. 1	Balance	√				56,803.00

Income Tax Payable   Account Number 20200

Date	Item	Post Ref	Debit	Credit	Balance Debit	Balance Credit
20XX						

Salaries Payable   Account Number 20300

Date	Item	Post Ref	Debit	Credit	Balance Debit	Balance Credit
20XX						

Cash Dividends Payable
Account Number 20400

Date	Item	Post Ref	Debit	Credit	Balance	
					Debit	Credit
20XX						

Interest Payable
Account Number 20500

Date	Item	Post Ref	Debit	Credit	Balance	
					Debit	Credit
20XX						

Property Tax Payable
Account Number 20600

Date	Item	Post Ref	Debit	Credit	Balance	
					Debit	Credit
20XX						

Note Payable
Account Number 26000

Date	Item	Post Ref	Debit	Credit	Balance	
					Debit	Credit
20XX						

Common Stock
Account Number 30100

Date	Item	Post Ref	Debit	Credit	Balance	
					Debit	Credit
20XX Dec. 1	Balance	√				100,000.00

Premium on Common Stock
Account Number 30200

Date	Item	Post Ref	Debit	Credit	Balance	
					Debit	Credit
20XX						

Retained Earnings
Account Number 35000

Date	Item	Post Ref	Debit	Credit	Balance Debit	Balance Credit
20XX Dec. 1	Balance	√				68,662.00

Donated Capital
Account Number 36000

Date	Item	Post Ref	Debit	Credit	Balance Debit	Balance Credit
20XX						

Income Summary
Account Number 40000

Date	Item	Post Ref	Debit	Credit	Balance Debit	Balance Credit
20XX						

Sales
Account Number 41000

Date	Item	Post Ref	Debit	Credit	Balance Debit	Balance Credit
20XX Dec. 1	Balance	√				475,445.00

Sales Discounts
Account Number 41500

Date	Item	Post Ref	Debit	Credit	Balance Debit	Balance Credit
20XX Dec. 1	Balance	√			4,000.00	

Sales Returns and Allowances

Account Number 41600

Date	Item	Post Ref	Debit	Credit	Balance Debit	Balance Credit
20XX Dec. 1	Balance	√			2,000.00	

Cost of Goods Sold

Account Number 51000

Date	Item	Post Ref	Debit	Credit	Balance Debit	Balance Credit
20XX Dec. 1	Balance	√			206,000.00	

Salaries Expense

Account Number 60100

Date	Item	Post Ref	Debit	Credit	Balance Debit	Balance Credit
20XX Dec. 1	Balance	√			133,685.00	

Utilities Expense

Account Number 60200

Date	Item	Post Ref	Debit	Credit	Balance Debit	Balance Credit
20XX Dec. 1	Balance	√			3,000.00	

Office Supplies Expense

Account Number 60300

Date	Item	Post Ref	Debit	Credit	Balance Debit	Balance Credit
20XX Dec. 1	Balance	√			2,000.00	

Advertisement Expense   **Account Number 60400**

Date	Item	Post Ref	Debit	Credit	Balance Debit	Balance Credit
20XX Dec. 1	Balance	√			7,000.00	

Depreciation Expense—Office Equipment   **60500**

Date	Item	Post Ref	Debit	Credit	Balance Debit	Balance Credit
20XX						

Depreciation Expense—Building   **Account Number 60600**

Date	Item	Post Ref	Debit	Credit	Balance Debit	Balance Credit
20XX						

Insurance Expense   **Account Number 60700**

Date	Item	Post Ref	Debit	Credit	Balance Debit	Balance Credit
20XX Dec. 1	Balance	√			2,750.00	

Uncollectible Accounts Expense   **Account Number 60800**

Date	Item	Post Ref	Debit	Credit	Balance Debit	Balance Credit
20XX Dec. 1	Balance	√			4,500.00	

Property Tax Expense   **Account Number 60900**

Date	Item	Post Ref	Debit	Credit	Balance Debit	Balance Credit
20XX Dec. 1	Balance	√			1,665.00	

Miscellaneous Expense   **Account Number 61000**

Date	Item	Post Ref	Debit	Credit	Balance Debit	Balance Credit
20XX Dec. 1	Balance	√			100.00	

Gain on Sale of Marketable Securities   **Account Number 61100**

Date	Item	Post Ref	Debit	Credit	Balance Debit	Balance Credit
20XX						

Interest Expense   **Account Number 61200**

Date	Item	Post Ref	Debit	Credit	Balance Debit	Balance Credit
20XX						

Amortization Expense—Organization Costs   **Account Number 61300**

Date	Item	Post Ref	Debit	Credit	Balance Debit	Balance Credit
20XX						

Income Tax   **Account Number 61400**

Date	Item	Post Ref	Debit	Credit	Balance Debit	Balance Credit
20XX						

Runners Corporation
Complete List of Accounts Receivable

Customer Number	Customer Name	Customer Street Address	Customer City, State	Customer Zip
2052	Active Sporting Stores	6500 Roosevelt Way	Seattle, WA	98104
2056	All Sporting	200 Mercer Street	Mercer Island, WA	98040
2057	Home Shoes Center	140 Lake Hills	Bellevue, WA	98009
2058	String Stores	1000 1st Avenue	Seattle, WA	98104
2050	Tog Sport Shop	2000 2nd Avenue	Woodinville, WA	98072
2055	True Sports Shop	126 12th Avenue South	Seattle, WA	98107

Accounts Receivable Ledger

Active Sporting Stores   **Customer #2052**

Date	Item	Journal Reference	Debit	Credit	Balance
20XX Nov. 1	Invoice # 6180	GJ or SJ	28,689		28,689

All Sporting   **Customer #2056**

Date	Item	Journal Reference	Debit	Credit	Balance
20XX Nov. 1	Invoice # 6192	GJ or SJ	4,000		4,000

Home Shoes Center   **Customer # 2057**

Date	Item	Journal Reference	Debit	Credit	Balance
20XX Nov. 1		GJ or SJ	13,150		13,150

North Shoes   **Customer # 2062**

Date	Item	Journal Reference	Debit	Credit	Balance
20XX					

String Stores   **Customer # 2058**

Date	Item	Journal Reference	Debit	Credit	Balance
20XX					

Tog Sport Shop   **Customer # 2050**

Date	Item	Journal Reference	Debit	Credit	Balance
20XX Feb. 1	Invoice # 6030	GJ or SJ	2,000		2,000

True Sports Shop   **Customer # 2055**

Date	Item	Journal Reference	Debit	Credit	Balance
20XX					

Runners Corporation
Complete List of Accounts Payable

Vendor Number	Vendor Name	Vendor Street Address	Vendor City, State	Vendor Zip
02	Hay Manufacturing Company	100 Marine Park View	New York, NY	10024
03	Hoot Manufacturing Company	300 Sutter Street	Los Angeles, CA	90015
04	Say Manufacturing Company	400 Bancroff Avenue	New York, NY	10024
05	Tic Manufacturing Company	132 NE 5th	Los Angeles, CA	90015
01	Tice Manufacturing Company	200 Westlake Avenue	Los Angeles, CA	90015

Accounts Payable Ledger

Hay Manufacturing Company   Vendor # 02

Date	Item	Journal Reference	Debit	Credit	Balance
20XX Nov. 17	P.O. # 3533	GJ or PJ		33,000	33,000

Hoot Manufacturing Company   Vendor # 03

Date	Item	Journal Reference	Debit	Credit	Balance
20XX Nov. 17	P.O. # 3532	GJ or PJ		18,000	18,000

Say Manufacturing Company   Vendor # 04

Date	Item	Journal Reference	Debit	Credit	Balance
20XX Nov. 21	P.O. # 3534	GJ or PJ		5,803	5,803

Tic Manufacturing Company   Vendor # 05

Date	Item	Journal Reference	Debit	Credit	Balance
20XX					

Tice Manufacturing Company   **Vendor # 01**

Date	Item	Journal Reference	Debit	Credit	Balance
20XX					

Runners Corporation
Schedule of Accounts Receivable
December 31, 20XX

Customer No.	Customer	Amount

Runners Corporation
Schedule of Accounts Payable
December 31, 20XX

Vendor No.	Supplier	Amount

RUNNERS CORPORATION
WORKSHEET
For Month Ended December 31, 20XX

Account Title	Trial Balance		Adjustments		Adjusted Trial Balance		Income Statement		Balance Sheet	
	Dr.	Cr.	Dr.	Cr.	Dr.	Cr.	Dr.	Cr.	Dr.	Cr.

RUNNERS CORPORATION
WORKSHEET
For Month Ended December 31, 20XX

Account Title	Trial Balance		Adjustments		Adjusted Trial Balance		Income Statement		Balance Sheet	
	Dr.	Cr.	Dr.	Cr.	Dr.	Cr.	Dr.	Cr.	Dr.	Cr.

RUNNERS CORPORATION
WORKSHEET
For Month Ended December 31, 20XX

Account Title	Trial Balance		Adjustments		Adjusted Trial Balance		Income Statement		Balance Sheet	
	Dr.	Cr.	Dr.	Cr.	Dr.	Cr.	Dr.	Cr.	Dr.	Cr.

Runners Corporation Income Statement For Year Ended December 31, 20XX		

Runners Corporation Statement of Retained Earnings For Year Ended December 31, 20XX		

Runners Corporation Balance Sheet December 31, 20XX			

Runners Corporation Statement of Cash Flows For Year Ended December 31, 20XX		

Runners Corporation Post-Closing Trial Balance December 31, 2009		
Account	Balance	
	Debit	Credit

Appendix B

Working with Accounting Software

Before you begin to work with PH General Ledger Software, QuickBooks Pro 2008 or 2009 or Peachtree Complete 2008 or 2009 you need to be familiar with your computer hardware and the Windows operating system. When you are running Windows, your work takes place on the desktop. Think of this area as resembling the surface of a desk. There are physical objects on your real desk, and there are windows and icons on the Windows desktop. There are minor differences between the various versions of Windows. The screens shown will reflect a typical Windows XP Desktop.

A mouse is an essential input device for all Windows applications. A mouse is a pointing device that assumes different shapes on your monitor as you move the mouse on your desk. According to the nature of the current action, the mouse pointer may appear as a small arrowhead, an hourglass, a double arrow, or a hand. There are five basic mouse techniques:

Click	To quickly press and release the left mouse button.
Double-click	To click the left mouse button twice in rapid succession.
Drag	To hold down the left mouse button while you move the mouse.
Point	To position the mouse pointer over an object without clicking a button.
Right-click	To quickly press and release the right mouse button.

The Windows XP Desktop

The following picture shows a typical opening Windows XP screen. Your desktop may be different, just as your real desk is arranged differently from those of your colleagues. Some of the items you will see on your desktop are:

♦ **Desktop icons:** Graphic representations of drives, files, and other resources. The desktop icons that display will vary depending on your computer setup.
♦ **Start button:** Clicking on the Start button displays the start menu and lets you start applications.
♦ **Taskbar:** Contains the Start button and other buttons representing open applications.

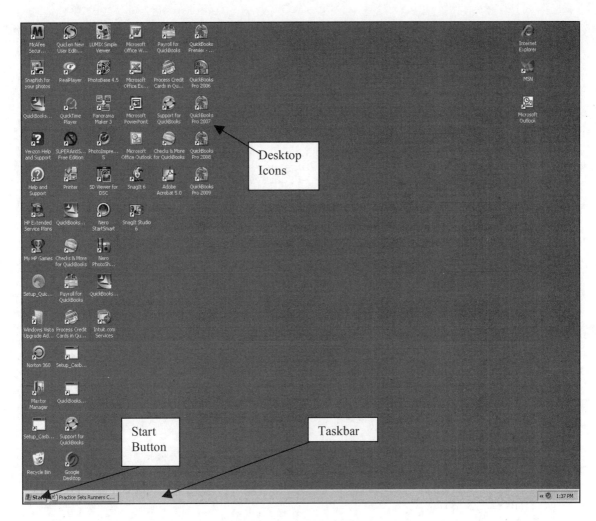

Windows XP Desktop

PH General Ledger Software

This section discusses several basic operations that you need to complete to install PH General Ledger program and the student data file for use in completing the computer workshop assignment. PH General Ledger Software has Help Content as well as a Quick Tour to become familiar with the features of the program.

Application Window

As you work with PH General Ledger a window containing three sections will appear on your desktop. In the upper left corner, the problem help displays. The upper right side of the window displays tabs designating the various windows available. The lower half of the window displays the General Journal.

When using a program, the window will show items or menus that are specific to the application that is in use. The name of the program and its menu bar will appear at the top of the application window. Regardless of the windows that are open on your desktop, most windows have certain elements in common. To see the following items, refer to the PH General Ledger window on the next page:

♦ **Minimize button:** Clicking on this button minimizes a window and displays it as a task button on the taskbar.

- ♦ **Maximize button:** Clicking on this button enlarges the window so that it fills the entire desktop. After you enlarge a window, the maximize button is replaced by a Restore button (a double box, not shown) that returns the window to the size it was before it was maximized.
- ♦ **Close button:** Clicking on this button will close the window.
- ♦ **Title bar:** Displays the name of the application.
- ♦ **Menu bar:** This window element lists the available menus for the window.
- ♦ **Drop-Down Menu:** Shows the options available under each menu option.
- ♦ **Highlighted (selected) Item:** The active selection in a Drop-Down Menu.
- ♦ **Standard Tool bar:** This window element displays the button commands used for the program.
- ♦ **Status bar:** A line of text at the bottom of many windows that gives more information about a field. If you are unsure of what to enter in a field, select it with your mouse and read the status bar.

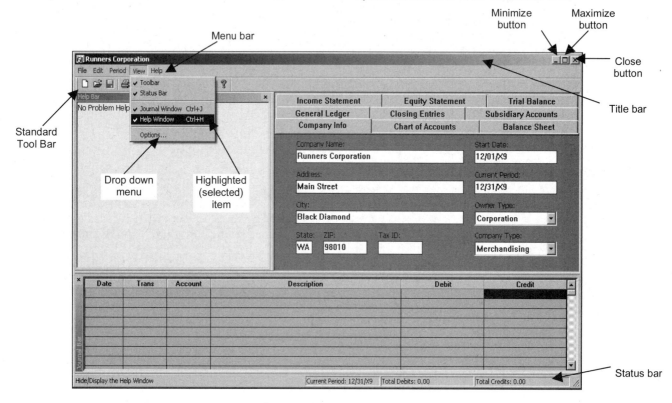

PH General Ledger

Dialog Boxes

A dialog box appears when additional information is needed to execute a command. There are different ways to supply that information; consequently, there are different types of dialog boxes. Most dialog boxes are for specific functions and tasks and require you to supply the data for that task. After you supply the needed information, you can choose a command button to carry out a command such as Print.

Other dialog boxes (see Print Dialog Box following) may require that choices be made, request additional information, provide warnings, or give messages indicating why a requested task cannot be accomplished.

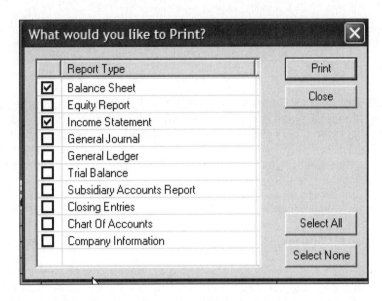

PH General Ledger Print Dialog Box

Using Menus

Commands are listed on menus, as shown below. Each item on the **Main Menu Bar** has its own menus, which are listed by selecting the menu. When a menu is displayed, choose a command by clicking on it or by typing the **Underlined Letter** to execute the command. You can also bypass the menu entirely if you know the **Keyboard equivalent** shown to the right of the command when the menu is displayed.
A **Dimmed Command** indicates that a command is not currently executable; some additional action has to be taken for the command to become available. Some commands are followed by **Ellipses** (...) to indicate that more information is required to execute the command. The additional information can be entered into a dialog box, which will appear immediately after the command has been selected.

PH General Ledger File Menu

Although PH General Ledger has five menu options available on the **Main Menu Bar**, most of your activities will involve the use of the Tab reports and general journal as well as the standard tool bar.

QuickBooks Pro 2008 or 2009:

Applications Window

As you work with QuickBooks Pro 2008 or 2009, you will use menus, navigation bars, and different centers. Usually, the Home Page is the center shown in the screen. From there, you may access the different areas of QuickBooks by clicking on an icon, a menu, or using a keyboard shortcut.

When using a program, the application window will show items or menus that are specific to the program that is in use. The name of the program and its menu bar will appear at the top of the application window. Regardless of the windows that are open on your desktop, most windows have certain elements in common. To see the following items, refer to the QuickBooks Pro 2008 or 2009 window shown:

♦ **Minimize button:** Clicking on this button minimizes a window and displays it as a task button on the taskbar.
♦ **Maximize button:** Clicking on this button enlarges the window so that it fills the entire desktop. After you enlarge a window, the maximize button is replaced by a Restore button (a double box, not shown) that returns the window to the size it was before it was maximized.
♦ **Close button:** Clicking on this button will close the window.
♦ **Title bar:** Displays the name of the application.
♦ **Menu bar:** This window element lists the available menus for the window.
♦ **Drop-Down Menu:** Shows the options available under each menu option.
♦ **Highlighted (selected) Item:** The active selection in a Drop-Down Menu.
♦ **The Home Page:** The Home Page offers quick access to tasks and information related to major QuickBooks areas.
♦ **The Navigation Bar:** The Navigation Bar on the toolbar provides one-click access to QuickBooks Centers and the Home Page.
♦ **Icon:** A small picture indicating a command
♦ **Keyboard Shortcut:** A combination of keystrokes that will give a command

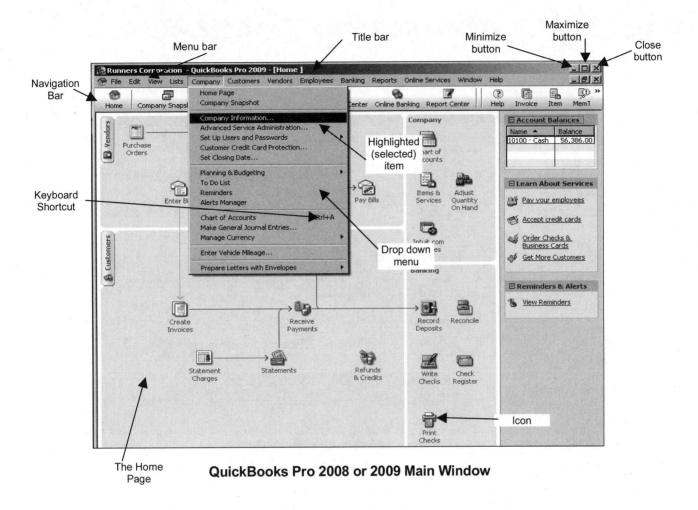

QuickBooks Pro 2008 or 2009 Main Window

Dialog Boxes

A dialog box appears when additional information is needed to execute a command. There are different ways to supply that information; consequently, there are different types of dialog boxes. Most dialog boxes are for specific functions and tasks and require you to supply the data for that task. After you supply the needed information, you can choose a command button to carry out a command such as to Save or Print. Some common items in a dialog box are:

◆ **Drop-down list arrow button:** A button with an arrow will generally bring up a pull-down menu of options for that field.
◆ **Text box:** When you move to an empty text box, an insertion point appears in the far left-hand side of the box. The text you type starts at the insertion point. If the box you move to already contains text, this text is selected (highlighted), and any text you type replaces it. You can also delete the selected text by pressing the DELETE or BACKSPACE key.
◆ **Command icons:** Click on a command icon to initiate an immediate action. The Print, Previous and Next buttons are common command buttons.
◆ **Magnifying glass button:** Click on this button to pull down a list of choices. Some fields will not show the magnifying glass until the field has been selected. (Not shown)
◆ **Calendar button:** Click on this button to bring up a calendar in order to select the date to be inserted in the field next to the button.

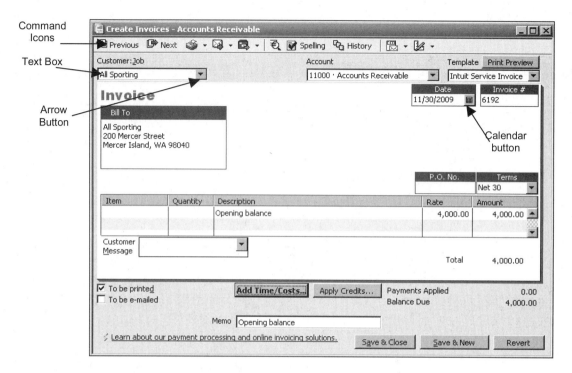

Command Icons

Text Box

Arrow Button

Calendar button

QuickBooks Pro 2008 or 2009 Invoice

Other dialog boxes may require that choices be made, request additional information, provide warnings, or give messages indicating why a requested task cannot be accomplished.

- ♦ **Highlighted (selected) item:** to highlight and/or select an item in a displayed list, click on the item. Some may require a double click to select. In the following example, highlighting an item in Report Area will bring up a list associated with that item in the Report List box. Highlighting an item in the Report List box will bring up a description in the Report Description box.
- ♦ **Scroll bar:** A bar that may appear at the bottom and/or right side of a window or dialog box if there is more text than can be displayed at one time within the window.
- ♦ **Scroll arrow:** A small arrow at the end of a scroll bar that you click on to move to the next item in the list. The top and left arrow scroll to the previous item; the bottom and right arrows scroll to the next item.
- ♦ **Scroll box:** A small box in a scroll bar. You can use the mouse to drag the scroll box left or right, or up or down. The scroll box indicates the relative position in the list.

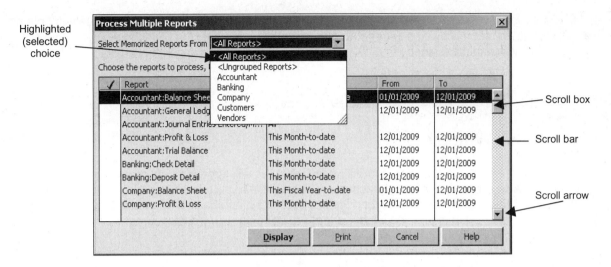

QuickBooks Pro 2008 or 2009 Process Multiple Reports

Using Menus

Commands are listed on menus. Each item on the **Main Menu Bar** has its own menu, which are listed by selecting the menu. When a menu is displayed, choose a command by clicking on it or by typing the **Underlined letter** to execute the command. You can also bypass the menu entirely if you know the **Keyboard equivalent** shown to the right of the command when the menu is displayed.

A **Dimmed command** indicates that a command is not currently executable; some additional action has to be taken for the command to become available. Some commands are followed by **Ellipses** (…) to indicate that more information is required to execute the command. Other commands have arrows, which indicate that there are several choices available for that command. Any additional information required can be entered into a dialog box, which will appear immediately after the command has been selected.

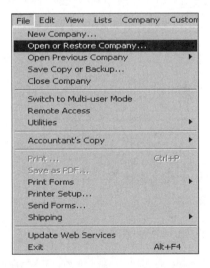

QuickBooks Pro 2008 or 2009 File Menu

Although QuickBooks has 13 menu options available on the **Main Menu Bar**, most of your activities will involve the **File Customers**, **Vendors**, **Employees**, **Banking**, or **Reports** menus. These menus contain all of our routine, day-to-day activities such as invoicing customers, paying vendors, generating payroll, et al. The **Lists** menu allows us to add, delete and edit customers, vendors, employees and default options, et al. The **Reports** menu allows us to generate the information contained in QuickBooks in a variety of formats including custom designed ones.

Peachtree Complete 2008 or 2009:

Applications Window

As you work with Peachtree Accounting two kinds of windows will appear on your desktop. The Main Menu window is where all activities in Peachtree will begin. An application window contains a running application. The name of the application and the application's menu bar will appear at the top of the application window. Regardless of the windows that are open on your desktop, most windows have certain elements in common.

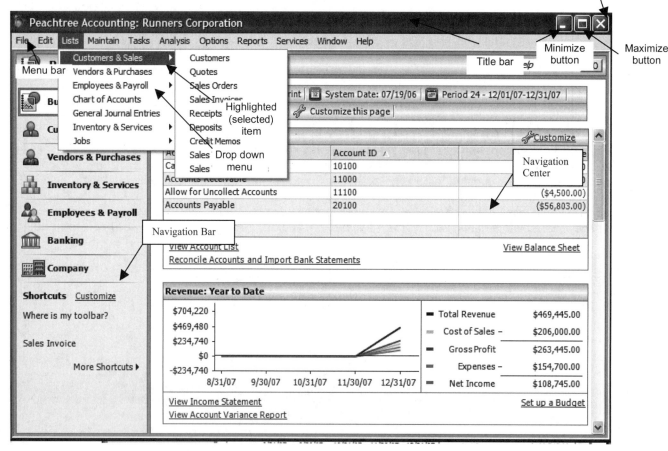

FIGURE B–9
Peachtree
Accounting
Main
Window

- ♦ **Minimize button:** Clicking on this button minimizes a window and displays it as a task button on the taskbar.
- ♦ **Maximize button:** Clicking on this button enlarges the window so that it fills the entire desktop. After you enlarge a window, the maximize button is replaced by a Restore button (a double box, not shown) that returns the window to the size it was before it was maximized.
- ♦ **Close button:** Clicking on this button will close the window.
- ♦ **Title bar:** Displays the name of the application.
- ♦ **Menu bar:** The menu bar provides drop-down lists of options.
- ♦ **Drop-Down Menu:** Shows the options available under each menu option.
- ♦ **Highlighted (selected) Item:** The active selection in a Drop-Down Menu.

98

- **Navigation Bar:** The Navigation Bar provides entry to the Navigation Centers. It also features a group of **Shortcuts**, links to Peachtree functions that you use on a regular basis.
- **Navigation Center:** These provide useful, at-a-glance information about areas of Peachtree such as Customer & Sales.

Dialog Boxes

A dialog box appears when additional information is needed to execute a command. There are different ways to supply that information; consequently, there are different types of dialog boxes. Most dialog boxes (see Fig. B-10) are for specific functions and tasks and require you to supply the data for that task. After you supply the needed information, you can choose a command button to carry out a command such as to Post or Print.

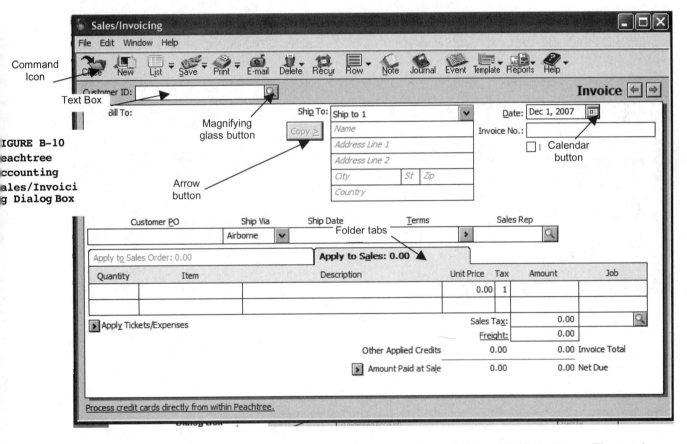

FIGURE B-10
Peachtree
Accounting
Sales/Invoici
ng Dialog Box

- **Folder tabs:** Some dialog boxes have multiple pages of entry fields available to them. These tabs allow you to switch between available screens.
- **Arrow button:** A button with an arrow will generally bring up a pull-down menu of options for that field.
- **Text box:** When you move to an empty text box, an insertion point appears in the far left-hand side of the box. The text you type starts at the insertion point. If the box you move to already contains text, this text is selected (highlighted), and any text you type replaces it. You can also delete the selected text by pressing the DELETE or BACKSPACE key.
- **Command icons:** Choose (click) on a command icon to initiate an immediate action such as carrying out or canceling a command. The Close, Print, and Process buttons are common command buttons.
- **Magnifying glass button:** Click on this button to pull down a list of choices. Some fields will not show the magnifying glass until the field has been selected.

♦ **Calendar button:** Click on this button to bring up a calendar in order to select the date to be inserted in the field next to the button.

Other dialog boxes (see Fig. B-11) may require that choices be made, request additional information, provide warnings, or give messages indicating why a requested task cannot be accomplished.

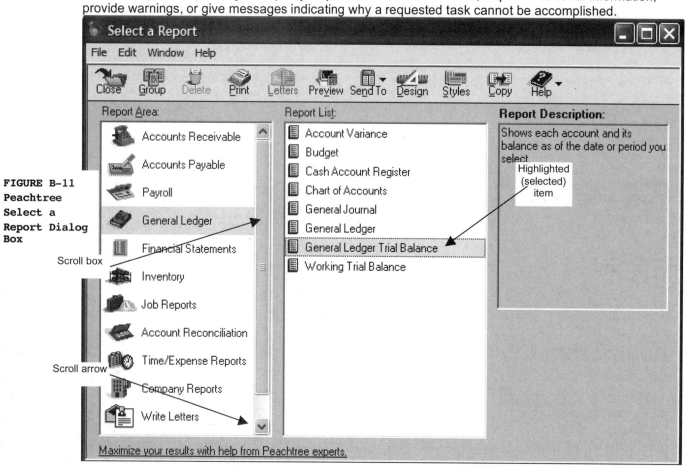

FIGURE B-11
Peachtree
Select a
Report Dialog
Box

♦ **Highlighted (selected) item:** to highlight and/or select an item in a displayed list, click on the item. Some may require a double-click to select. In figure B-11, highlighting an item in the Report Area will bring up a list associated with that item in the Report List box. Highlighting an item in the Report List box will bring up a description in the Report Description box.
♦ **Scroll bar:** A bar that may appear at the bottom and/or right side of a window or dialog box if there is more text than can be displayed at one time within the window.
♦ **Scroll arrow:** A small arrow at the end of a scroll bar that you click on to move to the next item in the list. The top and left arrow scroll to the previous item; the bottom and right arrows scroll to the next item.
♦ **Scroll box:** A small box in a scroll bar. You can use the mouse to drag the scroll box left or right, or up or down. The scroll box indicates the relative position in the list.

Using Menus

Commands are listed on menus, as shown in Figure B-12. Each item on the **Main Menu Bar** has its own menus, which are listed by selecting the menu. When a menu is displayed, choose a command by clicking on it or by typing the **Underlined letter** to execute the command. You can also bypass the menu entirely if you know the **Keyboard equivalent** shown to the right of the command when the menu is displayed.

A **Dimmed command** indicates that a command is not currently executable; some additional action has to be taken for the command to become available. Some commands are followed by **Ellipses** (...) to indicate that more information is required to execute the command. The additional information can be entered into a dialog box, which will appear immediately after the command has been selected.

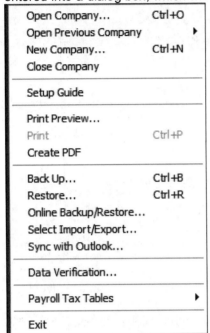

Open Company...	Ctrl+O
Open Previous Company	▶
New Company...	Ctrl+N
Close Company	
Setup Guide	
Print Preview...	
Print	Ctrl+P
Create PDF	
Back Up...	Ctrl+B
Restore...	Ctrl+R
Online Backup/Restore...	
Select Import/Export...	
Sync with Outlook...	
Data Verification...	
Payroll Tax Tables	▶
Exit	

FIGURE B-12
Peachtree
File Menu

Although Peachtree has 10 menu options available on the **Main Menu Bar**, most of your activities will involve the **Maintain**, **Tasks**, or **Reports** menus. The **Tasks** menu contains all of our routine, day-to-day activities such as invoicing customers, paying vendors, generating payroll, et al. The **Maintain** menu allows us to add, delete, and edit customers, vendors, employees and default options, et al. The **Reports** menu allows us to generate the information contained in Peachtree in a variety of formats including customer designed ones.

Appendix C

Transaction Corrections

Correcting Transactions Using PH General Ledger

Once a transaction is posted in PH General Ledger, the journal entry will be reflected in the accounting records. You will only be allowed to edit transactions that have not been posted. If you should detect an error while in the journal prior to posting you can quickly and easily correct the error prior to continuing with the transaction.

Correcting Unposted Errors
1. Using your mouse, click in the field that contains the error. This will highlight the selected text box information so that you can change it.
2. Select the correct information; then press enter. You may then use the mouse to click in the proper field.
3. If you have selected an incorrect account or any other type of look up information, use the drop-down menu to select the correct account or information. This will replace the incorrect account with the correct account.
4. To discard an entry and start over, click in the columns and press backspace. To delete the amount, click in the column and enter 0 (zero). To remove the zero just hit the backspace key.
5. To delete an entire transaction, click in any column of the transaction and click the Delete button from the toolbar.
6. Review the entry for accuracy after any editing corrections.
7. Complete the transaction by posting or printing.

Correcting Posted Errors
Enter a reversing entry to remove the incorrect entry and then reenter the correct entry.

Correcting Transactions Using QuickBooks Pro 2008 or 2009

Once a transaction is saved in QuickBooks Pro, the journal entry will be reflected in the accounting records. The program allows you to edit transactions easily. QuickBooks does have an electronic audit feature that creates an audit trail of all such changes. This feature of QuickBooks accounting is designed to ensure that a good audit trail of all transactions is constantly maintained within the program. This feature is turned on and off in the Company Navigator by clicking the **Preferences** icon, clicking **Accounting**, clicking **Use Audit** Trail, and clicking **OK**. In a real-world working situation, this feature would be turned on. Do not use this feature for training unless directed to so by your instructor.

If you should detect an error, while entering a transaction in a business document or journal, you can quickly and easily correct the error prior to continuing with the transaction.

Correcting Errors in Entries
1. Using your mouse, click in the field that contains the error. This will highlight the selected text box information so that you can change it.
2. Type the correct information; then press the TAB key to enter it. You may then either TAB to other fields needing corrections or again use the mouse to click in the proper field.
3. If you have selected an incorrect account or any other type of list information, use the drop-down list menu to select the correct information. This will replace the incorrect information with the correct information.

4. To discard an entry and start over, click the Edit menu, click Delete. You will be given a dialog box asking if you are sure you want to delete the transaction. Once you click OK, you will not be able to change your mind about deleting the transaction.
5. Review the entry for accuracy after any editing corrections.
6. Complete the transaction by clicking Save & New, Save & Close, or OK depending on the screen in use.

Correcting Posted Errors
Should you detect an error after you have saved (posted) the transaction, it can be corrected quickly and easily. The only additional step needed to correct a posted transaction is to find it and bring it up on your screen.

To locate a transaction for correction, you may
1. Click on the appropriate icon for a business document and click Previous until you get to the incorrect document.
2. Use QuickBooks's Find feature to locate a business document, amount, account, customer, vendor, item, date, etc.
3. Prepare a Journal Report. The Journal displays every transaction that has been entered in QuickBooks in a debit/credit format. When the report is on the screen, point to the line containing the item for correction. The cursor will turn into a magnifying glass with a Z in the center Select the line for correction by double-clicking the mouse cursor. QuickBooks will go to the location for the transaction entry for correction. Looking at a General Journal report under the Reports menu your screen will look like this:

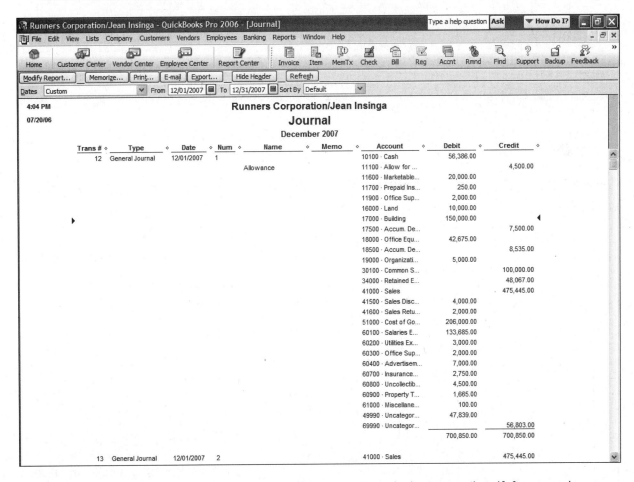

By double-clicking on any selected line, you can bring up that particular transaction. If, for example, we double-click the selection from figure C-2, we are presented with the following:

Figure C-2
Cash
Account
Transaction

We could edit any field of this entry and click Record to save the change. For other types of transactions, the procedures that were presented for correcting unposted transactions can now be applied.

Correcting Transactions using Peachtree Complete Accounting 2008 or 2009

Once a transaction is posted in Peachtree Complete Accounting 2008 or 2009, the journal entry will be reflected in the accounting records. You will however, be allowed to edit transactions due to the way the program has been configured for you. Peachtree does have an electronic audit feature that would not allow you to make corrections without creating an audit trail of all such changes. This feature of Peachtree Complete Accounting 2008 or 2009 is designed to ensure that a good audit trail of all transactions is constantly maintained within the program. This feature is turned on and off in the Company Information of the Maintain menu option. In a real world working situation, this feature would be turned on. Unless your instructor has you turn this feature on, you will be able to correct errors quickly and easily without creating a record of these corrections.

If you should detect an error while in any of Peachtree's input screens prior to posting or printing, you can quickly and easily correct the error prior to continuing with the transaction.

1.   Using your mouse, click in the field that contains the error. This will highlight the selected text box information so that you can change it.
2.   Type the correct information; then press the TAB key to enter it. You may then either TAB to other fields needing corrections or again use the mouse to click in the proper field.
3.   If you have selected an incorrect account or any other type of look up information, use the pull-down menu to select the correct account or information. This will replace the incorrect account with the correct account.

4. To discard an entry and start over, click on the Delete icon. You will not be given the opportunity to verify this step so be sure you want to delete the transaction before selecting this option. This option may not be available on every input screen.
5. Review the entry for accuracy after any editing corrections.
6. Complete the transaction by posting or printing.

Should you detect an error after you have posted the transaction, it can still be quickly and easily corrected. The only additional step needed to correct a posted transaction is to find it and bring it up on your screen.

Correcting Posted Errors

Generate an on-screen report which will contain the document needing correction. As an example, a sales invoice can be found in an Aged Receivables Report, an Invoice Register, or a Sales Journal. A General Journal entry can be found in a General Journal or a General Ledger report.

Select the line containing the item needing correction by single-clicking the mouse cursor. This will place a blue box around the line and the cursor will turn into a magnifying glass with a Z in the center. Looking at a Cash Receipts Journal report under the Reports menu, your screen will look like this:

Figure C-1 Cash Receipts Journal

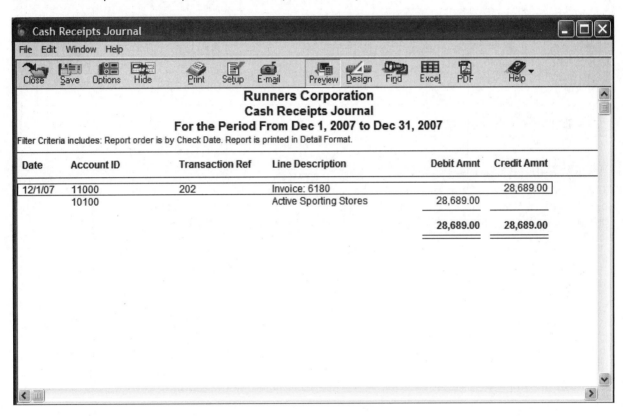

By double-clicking on any selected line, you can bring up that particular transaction. If, for example, we double-click the selection from figure C-1, we are presented with the following:

Figure C-2
Receipts

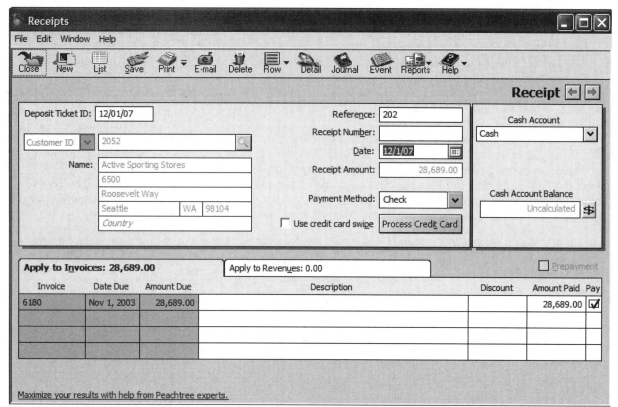

We could edit any field of this entry and Post it again. The procedure that was presented for correcting an unposted transaction can now be applied. You can experiment with this feature in the sample company if your program has Bellwether Garden Supply sample company installed.

Appendix D

How to Repeat or Restart an Assignment and Using the Backup of Company Data files

There are several reasons why you might wish to access a backup copy of a company's data files. For example, you may not have printed a required report in an assignment before advancing the period to a new month or before adding additional transactions. You may have several errors and simply want to start an assignment over or to a point prior to the errors rather than correct the many mistakes.
If you backup your data using a different filename each day, you will the option of restoring from any of these files. It would be wise to indicate in your text the point at which you created each backup so you will know what transactions have been completed at each of the backup's dates.

Backing up a File in PH General Ledger

PH General Ledger has the capability to quickly and easily back up your data to protect against accidental loss.

1. Click **File**
2. Click **Save As**
3. Enter the **filename**
4. Click **Save**

PH General Ledger will save your data files to any drive or path you specify including a floppy drive. It defaults to the location where the program files are stored and specifically to the folder where the company files are kept. Use the **Save In** drop-down menu to save the files to a location specified by your instructor. This could be a network drive, a student floppy drive or even the local hard drive. Click **Save** to complete the process. You now have a back up copy of your data. You should consider saving each and every day to protect yourself against possible loss.

Restoring Company Data Files

You always have the option to repeat an assignment for additional practice or start over on an assignment. You simply open the saved file.

Backing up a File in QuickBooks Pro 2008 or 2009

QuickBooks Pro Accounting has the capability to quickly and easily backup your data to protect against accidental loss. To do this, you must have opened the file of the company you wish to backup. Let's say we wish to backup Runners Corporation.
1. Click the **File** menu
2. Click **Save Copy or Back Up**.
3. Click **Backup copy**, click **Next**

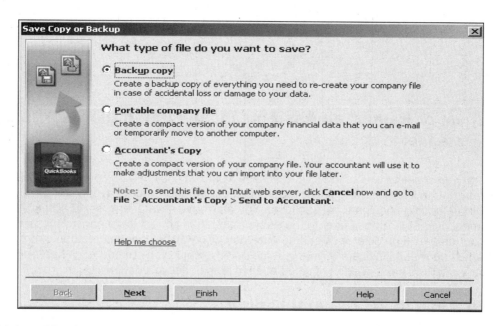

3. Click **Local backup**, click **Next**

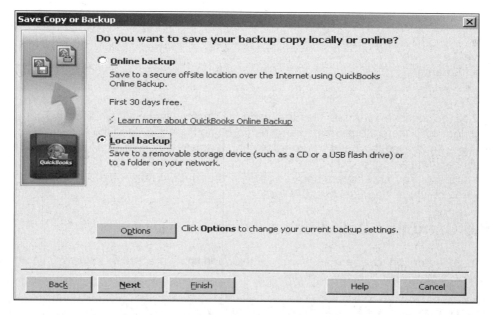

4. Click **Save it now**, click **Next**
5. Select the storage location for Save in: and enter the name of the backup file, click **Save**. QuickBooks will save your data files into one compressed .qbb file to any drive or path you specify.

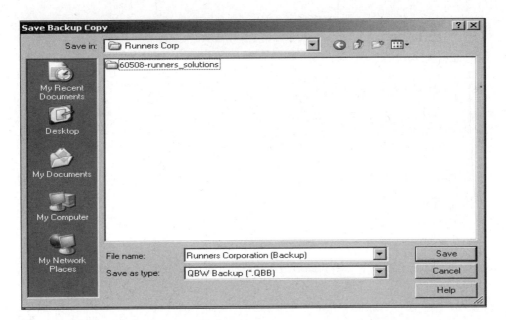

6. You are now presented with a Backup Complete dialog box for the Runners Corporation. Click **OK** to complete the process.

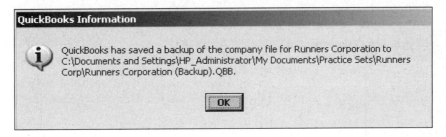

You now have a back up of your data. You should consider saving each and every day to protect yourself against possible loss. You do not have to accept the name QuickBooks Pro assigns and you can use a name with more meaning to you.

Restoring Company Data Files

You always have the option to repeat an assignment for additional practice or start over on an assignment. You simply restore the company files back to their original state using the Runners Corp [Backup] created at the start of the assignment. The procedure for restoring a file is very similar to creating a backup. To restore Runners Corporation:

1. Open the company using the **Open** feature from the **File** menu option.
2. Click **Restore a backup copy**, click **Next**

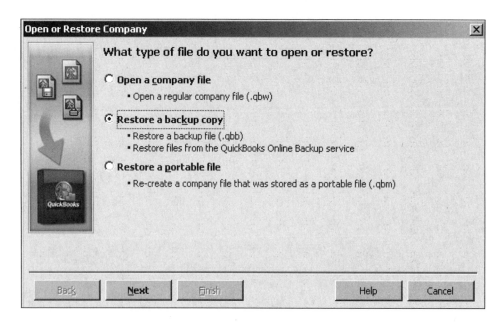

3. Click **Local backup**, click **Next**

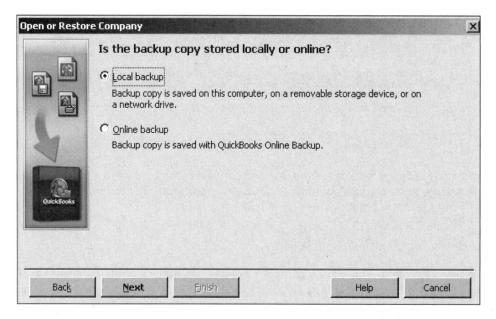

4. Select the storage location for Look in: and click the name of the backup file, click **Open**

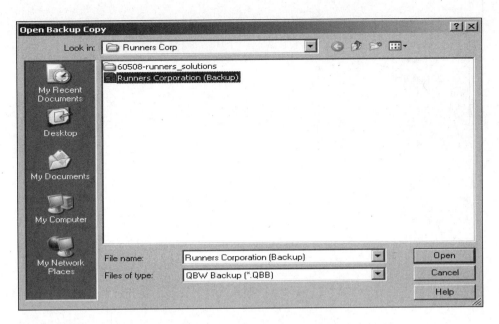

5. Click **Next** on the screen "Where do you want to restore the file?"

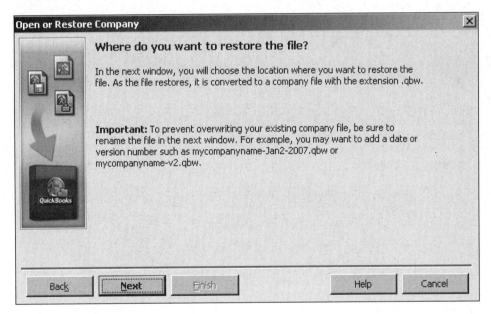

6. Select the storage location for Save in: and enter the name of the company file, click **Save**.

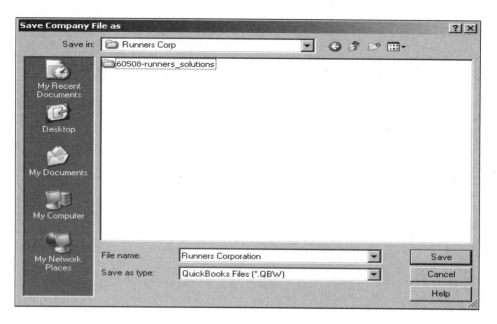

7.   If you already have a file named Runners Corporation in the Save in: location, QuickBooks will ask you if you want to replace it. Click **Yes**

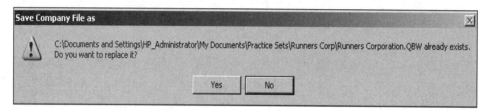

8.   To make sure you want to replace the file, QuickBooks requires you to type **YES** in the Delete Entire File dialog box, and click **OK**.

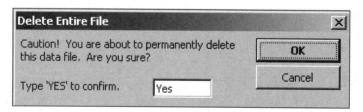

9.   When the file has been restored you will get a dialog box stating that your data has been restored successfully. Click **OK**

Backing up a File in Peachtree Complete Accounting

Peachtree Complete Accounting has the capability to quickly and easily back up your data to protect against accidental loss.

1. To backup A-1 Photography, open the company using the **Open** feature from the **File** menu option.
2. Select **Back Up** from the **File** menu option.
3. Click in the box next to Include company name in the backup file name. This will make Peachtree use A-1 Photography in the filename it selects for the backup. (You could also use this dialogue box to have Peachtree provide a reminder at periodic intervals.)
4. Click Back Up.

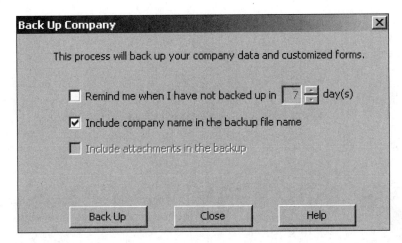

4. The Save Backup for the A-1 Photography—Your Name as: dialog box is displayed.
5. Verify the location for **Save in:** (Peachtree will save your data files into one compressed .ptb file to any drive or path you specify. It defaults to the location where the company files are kept. Use the **Save in** pull-down menu to save the files to a location specified by your instructor. This could be a network drive, a USB drive, or even the local hard drive.)
6. Enter the **File name**

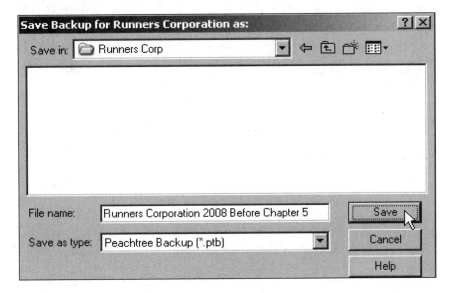

7. Click **Save**

You now have a backup of your data. You should consider saving each and every day to protect yourself against possible loss. Unless otherwise instructed, Peachtree will use the date as part of the backup's name so you could have a separate backup for each day. You do not have to accept the name Peachtree assigns and you can use a name with more meaning to you.

In addition to a daily backup, you should create a backup file at different points:
>Before Adjusting Entries
>After Adjusting Entries
>After Closing a Period

Restoring Company Data Files

You always have the option to repeat an assignment for additional practice or start over on an assignment. You simply restore the sample company files back to their original state using the Backup created at the start of the assignment. The procedure for restoring a file is very similar:

1. Open A-1 Photography.
2. Select Restore from the File menu option. This will bring up the Restore Wizard dialogue box.
3. Verify the Location of the file. (If the Location is incorrect, click the Browse button to locate the correct folder.)
4. When the appropriate file is found, click Next to continue through the wizard to select the exact backup file to restore.

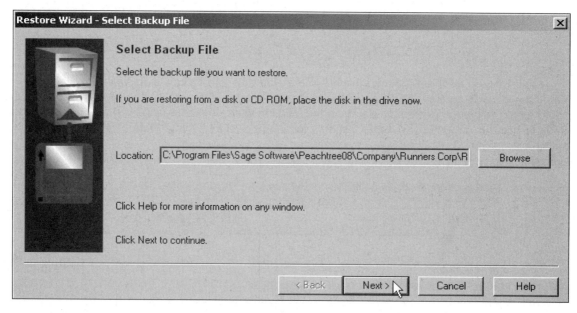

5. Complete the Select Company windows, click Next

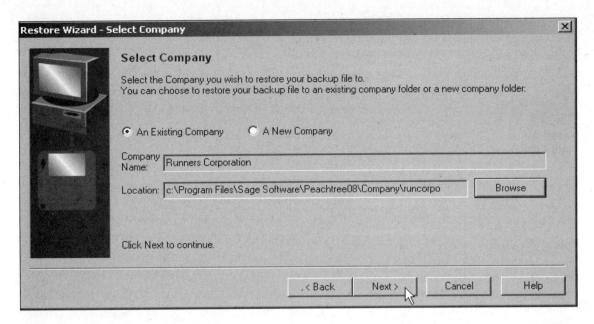

6. Select the Peachtree files you want to restore

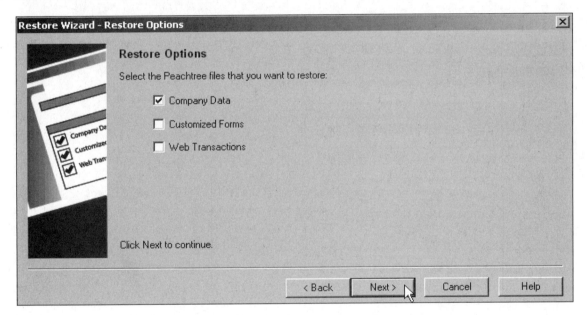

7. Verify the information on the Confirmation screen, click Finish.

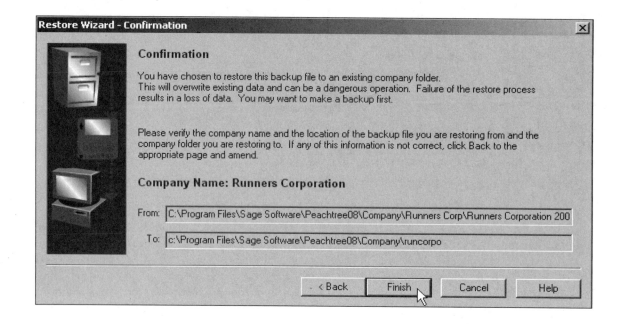

Restore Wizard - Confirmation ☒

Confirmation

You have chosen to restore this backup file to an existing company folder.
This will overwrite existing data and can be a dangerous operation. Failure of the restore process results in a loss of data. You may want to make a backup first.

Please verify the company name and the location of the backup file you are restoring from and the company folder you are restoring to. If any of this information is not correct, click Back to the appropriate page and amend.

Company Name: Runners Corporation

From: | C:\Program Files\Sage Software\Peachtree08\Company\Runners Corp\Runners Corporation 200

To: | c:\Program Files\Sage Software\Peachtree08\Company\runcorpo

[< Back] [Finish] [Cancel] [Help]